"Our Father, Who Art in Heaven,
Hallowed Be Thy Name . . ."

"Blessed Art Thou,
Oh Lord Our God . . ."

"In the Name of Allah,
the Compassionate, the Merciful . . ."

The great religions come to life
through photographs, a poetic text,
and the personal experiences of a world
traveler who has worshiped with lamas,
sat with Hindu sadhus, and answered
the muezzin's call to prayer.

THE FIVE GREAT RELIGIONS

"Describes the central concepts and historical developments of Hinduism, Buddhism, Judaism, Islam and Christianity with obvious feeling and understanding."
—American Library Association *Booklist*

"Particularly strong on Eastern religions—the incredible richness of Hinduism, the teachings of Buddha, the nonverbal character of Zen."
—*Kirkus Reviews*

EDWARD RICE

photographs by the author

THE FIVE GREAT
RELIGIONS

BANTAM BOOKS · TORONTO · NEW YORK · LONDON

VLM 10 (VLR 8–12)

IL 8 +

THE FIVE GREAT RELIGIONS

*A Bantam Book / published by arrangement with
Four Winds Press*

PRINTING HISTORY

*Four Winds Press edition published October 1973
2nd printing . . . . . November 1973*

Bantam edition / February 1977

ISBN 0-553-10106-4

CONTENTS

INTRODUCTION   1

HINDUISM   7

BUDDHISM   51

JUDAISM   105

ISLAM   149

CHRISTIANITY   195

INDEX   235

INTRODUCTION

 I write as a person brought up in one of the Western—that is, Judaeo-Christian—traditions. But this is not to say that I write as a Western, Christian partisan. Nor am I writing from the common point of view that divides the world into Christian and "non-Christian" religions. Over and over again as I studied and read and talked to people and wrote about Hinduism, Buddhism, Judaism and Islam, I was struck by the tremendous cosmological point of view of each. As I studied Hinduism and traveled in India, I felt absorbed in the Hindu view of the world, in the tremendous touch of the Divine that envelops, consumes, devours, until man and the Divine are One, in a constant flow of the soul from one level to another. And moving from Hinduism into Buddhism, I could experience the Buddhist message that life is but suffering and ignorance, not as punishment, the result of a divine or cosmic wrath, but because we as men are ignorant.

Judaism brought me into the eternal dialogue between man and God and the world, the I/Thou, the I/It relationship which becomes even more pronounced, more personal, in later aspects of Judaism, when the vision of God has changed from one of a sometimes frightful, punitive Power to the benevolent warmth of His eternal Friendship. Islam took me into the great gulf, the stark desert that is not only physical but also theological and psychological, which separates man from God: man is stripped of all but his ability to pray, calling upon the fierceness of the Divine Love. And Christianity, with its magnificent promise of God Incarnate, of a vision at once realized and at the same time betrayed not by God but by man, brings us face to face with man's love, arrogance, cruelty, creativity, complacency, and deception, all consumed in a quest for God.

I have written about Christianity in terms different from the others. The section on the major religion of the West is presented as an appendix in the light of the other world religions. For one thing the West has divided the world into Christian and non-Christian religions. It would strike us funny if a Buddhist parceled out man's religious beliefs into "Buddhist and non-Buddhist." Many devout, practicing Christians might even resent the distinction. Yet I have come across an abundance of Christian material which treats all other religions, with the exception of Judaism, as "pagan," "heathen," "idolatrous," and so on. I will expand upon this point in the last chapter.

At the same time I hope to make it clear that I am not favoring one religion over another, nor am I seeking to find an amalgam, as groups like the Theosophists and Bahai have hoped to do. I am not telling the Christian to become a Hindu or a Buddhist, or the Jew or the Muslim to become a Christian. What I have tried to do is to present Hinduism, Buddhism, Judaism, and Islam each in its own terms, and to reflect Christianity against them.

I have tended to stress the mystical aspects and traditions of all the religions (they are basic in Hinduism and Buddhism and need no extra emphasis) because, while mystics may quantitatively be a minority, they form the inner "soul" of all religions. If we are not looking for "quality" in a religion, then religion exists more as a sociological and cultural force than as a valid means of establishing a relationship between man and the Divine. In both Hinduism and Buddhism mysticism in some form or other is the goal of ordinary life, though naturally, man, being weak, often fails in the search. Though not all men can follow the path, the search for the interior life is considered normal and acceptable.

In the monotheistic religions—Judaism, Islam, and Christianity—mysticism, it must be admitted, is not the conventional Way except for a certain few. In these faiths the mystic has often been suspect, and sometimes has even been persecuted. In death, the mystic usually achieves a certain respectability and may even be sainted. But the live mystic is always a threat. His quiet devotion, piety, asceticism, gentleness; his otherworldliness and eschewing of such necessities as shelter, food, clothing and money; his disregard for social position, rank and caste, are compelling arguments for his beliefs and are dangers to orthodoxy, particularly when the institutions must follow a different path.

We find that mystics often exhibit the most suspicious of all traits: true tolerance and acceptance of others. Over and over again, in my work here and abroad, in talking to people I consider to be mystics or as being on the way to a state of mysticism, I encountered the attitude that there is "no such thing as caste," that "all men are brothers," that there is "no distinction between Hindu, Muslim and Christian," "no Jew or Gentile." In other words, the mystic goes beyond secular confession into the Absolute, and in the Absolute all men are One.

We must try to approach each religion on its own terms, not ours. The reader cannot dismiss Hinduism as "pagan" because of "all those gods," nor Buddhism as atheistic because it does not even entertain the concept of a Prime Mover. Nor can he dismiss Judaism as an unfulfilled preliminary of Christianity, and Islam as a weak, unformed and slightly heathen relative. And finally, the reader should not write off Christianity because Christians have failed to be Christian.

What is asked is an open mind and a reflective mind. In each reader's receptiveness he may find some glimmer of the Ground of All Being according to his own wishes, will, inclination and background.

Hinduism

 A void. The universe is enveloped in darkness, unperceived, undistinguishable, undiscovered, unknowable, sunk in sleep.

Then the irresistible, the self-existent Lord, undiscerned, who causes this universe with the five elements and all other things to become discernible, was manifested.

He who is beyond cognizance of senses, subtle, undiscernible and eternal, and is the essence of all beings, and inconceivable, shone forth.

Desiring, he seeks to produce various creatures from his own body. He first created the waters and deposited them as a seed. This seed became a golden egg, resplendent as the sun in which he himself was born as Brahma, the progenitor of the world.

Having continued a year in the egg, the Lord divides it into two parts by mere thought. With these two shells he forms the heaven and the earth, and in the middle he placed the sky, the eight regions, and the eternal abode of the waters.

Thus the origin of the earth and the universe according to Manu, the (mythical) sage of the Hindus.

Govind and I are sitting in a tiny white-washed room in a house high above the Hanumanghat in Benares, the most sacred of all Indian cities. Far below us is the Ganges, the most sacred of all Indian rivers, and perhaps of all the rivers of the world. It is now sunset, a most holy hour. There are pilgrims bathing in the river; we can hear their voices faintly. Nearby is a temple to Hanuman, the monkey god. Hanuman's devotion to the Lord Rama (whose name is synonymous in northern India with that of the Absolute and Almighty) is upheld as a model of the devotion every man should have for God. A small bell calls the worshippers together, and some of the bathers come up from the river, fresh and clean and carrying flowers. Along the northern side of the Ganges in Benares are the ghats; they are stone steps or ledges, piled with temples, palaces, mansions, and the homes and hovels of ordinary people. The northern bank is sacred because the Lord Gautama Buddha lived there, and preached his first sermon at Sarnath, a few miles away. (Thus began a daughter religion to Hinduism, Buddhism, which eventually grew to become the major faith of much of Asia.) The southern bank is flat and practically barren, since it has no sacred meaning and thus there is no reason to live there. Indians, especially Hindus, are in love with the sacred, in a way Westerners can rarely understand and often think sacrilegious. A French writer, Henri Michaux, who traveled through India in 1929, called Hindus "the people of the absolute, a radically religious people."

Dawn is the most sacred moment of the day. Along the holy rivers and waterways, people bathe and pray, perform their sacred rites, wash their utensils and clothes. The man with

the raised arms is a worshipper of the god Surya, the sun, honored as the center of creation and the source of life, of warmth and of all knowledge.

Michaux wrote that the Hindu is "greedy for God. One pictures the Hindu as leeches on God's surface."

My friend Govind is about twenty-six, university educated, and is caught between the two worlds of traditional India and the modern West. He had been trying to take stock of himself in an attempt to find his place in the chaos of modern life, which is striking young Indians as severely as it is young Americans. The conversation shifts to religion. Govind meditates daily, and believes in "equality, purity and universal love." We discuss religious experience in Govind's terms, not mine as a Westerner, and they may seem esoteric to the Christian and Jewish reader. Govind, deeply moved, settles into the lotus position, with his legs crossed beneath him (in India one normally sits on the floor) and remarks: "On my arms is Brahman, in my chest Hanuman, in my stomach Kali, and on top of my head Shiva—I can feel him there, he is real–and in my heart Christ."

Briefly defined (though everything in India is extremely complex) Brahman is the sacred supreme power, reality, knowledge, the infinite, intelligence, bliss; Kali, the Great Mother who devours in order that a new age may be born; Shiva, the reconciler of all opposites (he is both male and female, creator and destroyer, terrible and mild, evil and good, eternal rest and ceaseless activity). To Govind all the powers of the Hindu pantheon are embodied in Christ. But this is not to say that Govind is about to become a Christian. He is led to Christ only to draw

Pilgrims to Darjeeling in northern India watch the sun break over the Himalayas. In the distance they can see Mount Everest for a few moments before the fog moves in. Mountains, apparently inanimate, are believed to contain hidden spirits. According to the Kalika Purana, an ancient religious work, "rivers and mountains may take the forms they wish."

Christ into Hinduism. He sees no conflict and no contradiction. He embraces everything, all, at the same moment. It is this all-encompassing outlook that gives Hinduism a special character, which is at the same time both satisfying and confusing.

Govind adds: "If Christ should lead me, I would become a Christian." I ask him what his family would say (they are very strict Hindus). "Christ would lead them to understand." Michaux remarked that Westerners are often hurt by the familiarity with which Hindus talk about Christ; they consider him "one of us," an Asian. But Govind could become "Christian" without being any the less Hindu, if he wished. (This is not to say that other Hindus have not made the decision on an either/or basis.)

We go outside to look at the river in the dusk. The moon has risen: it is full, orange, erotic, and within touch. We talk about it with a young man who appears out of the dark; he too is a student but his face is painted with the trident of Shiva. Just a short while before there had been another American landing on the moon. Reaction in India (and elsewhere in Asia) was interesting. Some people accepted the American accomplishment as fact, as did Govind and his friend, but others thought it was just a story, a fable. Indians had been there first; the Scriptures said so. Some people believed there were two moons: the one we could see where the Americans had landed, and the real one, the moon of the holy books, which was the true moon but invisible. And then a large number of people claimed that the astronauts could not have landed upon any moon, since it is sacred. God would have destroyed them for their impious act.

What I am trying to convey to the reader is that to begin to comprehend Hinduism (and Buddhism as we will see, and to some extent even Islam) we need to dislocate the mind, to relocate it in another milieu, another climate, geography, time. Hinduism is a religion of heat, of the burning sun, of parched lands and broad sluggish rivers, of monsoon rains and famine, of riches and cultures and civilizations that span uncounted ages. Hinduism is lost in the mists of the ancient past. A thousand years before Abraham received the Covenant from God and became the father of nations, Hinduism already possessed the core of what it was to become. One measures Hinduism by millennia, not by centuries. Hinduism is a primordial religion. It "always was." There has been no "founder," no key or pivotal figure, like Abraham, Moses, Buddha, Christ or Muhammad, to give either a greater dimension to what already existed or to break sharply with the past to find a new vision of the eternal dialogue between God and man. Hinduism has been likened to a great river: it may change course, it may wander, but it is still the one great body drawing upon tributaries by the hundred, absorbing them into the vast current that has borne souls by the billions since the dawn

Brahma is the Immense Being. He has four faces—three are seen here, the fourth is directly behind the frontal view—and is seated upon a lotus. He is the source of all knowledge. He has no beginning. But in these times his power as preserver is being taken over by Vishnu and as destroyer by Shiva; and in the popular imagination his role has been usurped by Sakti, the Female Principle, who combines both aspects of destroyer and preserver as Energy. Brahma has four arms, and of the four heads it might be said that he once had five but the fifth was destroyed by the fire from Shiva's Third Eye.

of time. Even the greatest change of all in Hinduism, the fusing of the Vedic Aryan beliefs of the nomads who entered India from the northwest, took some nineteen hundred years, from 2500 B.C. to 600 B.C. This is as long as the entire history of Christianity.

India has "always" been inhabited by mankind. It had civilizations so old that they have been buried longer than those of the Babylonians, Hittites, Assyrians, and Egyptians. Cities have been recently uncovered which were the equal of ancient Rome in grandeur and may be five thousand years old. The archeological evidence that is being dug up only now shows that they had a high level of civilization, with well-developed industry, agricultural holdings, urban planning, brilliant cultural achievements, and firmly established religious beliefs. Two of the great Hindu deities, Shiva and Vishnu, were already being worshipped when the Aryans arrived.

The Aryans (the name Arya means noble) were part of the great wave of migrations that crossed into Iran, Europe, and the Middle East over a two-thousand-year period. In India, the civilizations they attacked were of a higher level than their own, which was that of nomadic warriors. They pushed back the indigenous inhabitants, killed them off, or made slaves of them. An early Vedic hymn says the Aryans were blond and fair-skinned, the inhabitants of the land they were despoiling, black-skinned. There was repression and murder, and over a long period, a slow mixing which finally pro-

A meeting of holy men from all over India—the Apple-Rose-Tree-Island in the ancient phrase—gather in a huge tent at Benares. They wear yellow shawls on which are imprinted red Hindi characters, Shri Ram, Lord God.

duced the civilization now known as Indian. The Aryans fused their own religious beliefs, which were akin to those of the Greeks, Romans, and Scandinavians, onto the primordial religion of the conquered people. It was a long process: There was no sudden flash, no deep inner experience, no awakening on the part of an individual to bring a new vision to the primordial beliefs. It was just the vast river, growing and deepening with ever-freshening tributaries.

The religious system which eventually came to be called Hinduism is not only a highly complex religious, theological, and philosophical structure, but a moral, social, ethical, and cultural one as well, which lays down codes of behavior for the individual's daily life. The religious and philosophical themes grapple with the great issues: God and man, time and eternity, the soul, rebirth, existence, duty, and fate. The moral and social codes not only tell a man how to handle his ordinary life in the most ethical and proper way, but also how he is to dress, how he is to bathe and defecate, what food he can eat or not eat, with whom he may associate, and even how close or far he may stand in relation to another person. Today many of these codes are in abeyance, and the complex theological systems have rarely touched the ordinary householder, but Hinduism is still an active and vital religious system. Directly or indirectly it forms the ancestral faith of something like half the people of the world, in India in the form of orthodox Hinduism, and in Asia through its offspring, Buddhism. By means of some slight but effective Buddhist influences in the past, it even has affected Judaism, Christianity, and Islam.

The social framework in which Hin-

duism is set is the caste system. Like many of the great races of mankind, Hindus believe they are of divine origin. They claim descent from Brahma, the Creator. The four primary divisions or castes believe they have sprung from parts of his body: the Brahmans (the priestly caste, which roughly corresponds to the Levites of the Jews) from his head; the Kshatriyas (warriors) from his arms; the Vaisayas (traders and agricultural workers) from his thighs; and the Sudras (menial workers) from his feet. There is also a large group, the Panchamas (fifth caste), more normally known as untouchables, because they are (or were) literally that, being considered so far below any caste of Hinduism that a higher caste Hindu would be seriously polluted if he should touch or be touched by one, or be served food cooked by an untouchable, or even if he allowed one to come within a certain distance. In his effort to help the untouchables gain admission to Indian society, Mahatma Gandhi called them "harijans"—the children of God. But by whatever name, despite legislation .to the contrary, they still remain outside and below the four main castes, performing the most abject work as sweepers and latrine cleaners, leather workers, and scavengers, or doing whatever other tasks would "pollute" caste Hindus. The vast majority of Hindus are either Sudras or untouchables, and the duty of all the lower castes, as might be expected, is to serve the Brahmans, the head, who (in theory) set and administer the rules.

In Bangladesh a member of the Hindu minority worships at a tiny shrine. He has placed his hand on his head to call God down from heaven.

Over the ages the castes have split into a number of subcastes, with some two or three thousand in all. The origins of caste are complicated and obscure. They are partly religious, partly social and economic, partly racial or occupational. Castes began to develop after the Aryan migrations, when the invaders tried to control the conquered by giving each racial, functional, or religious group its own niche in the emerging society.

It is birth that defines a man's caste. Everyone is born into a preordained station in life according to the divine plan. His current birth is determined by his actions in the past. A man accepts caste as part of his faith. Few attempt to pass themselves off as members of a higher caste: a man cannot pretend to be what he is not. Since the Hindu believes in being born again, living a lie in the present would jeopardize future reincarnation. One moves upward by leading a good life.

Reincarnation is basic to Hinduism. This belief in a rebirth on earth is a strict directive, a firm control over a man's actions, though it is obvious that not every man can follow such a path. On two occasions Hindu sadhus (or holy men) have read my horoscope in the light of certain sacred books and told me that in a previous existence I had been a high-caste Hindu, but had sinned and thus was reborn as a foreigner. I was advised to make certain sacrifices to the gods, and to lead a virtuous life and if I were lucky I might

Some eight million wandering holy men, commonly called sadhus, wander about India and its neighboring countries. This sadhu has come to Kathmandu in Nepal. He wears a tilak of sandalwood paste on his forehead.

be reborn a Hindu again. Thus, unfortunates like women, foreigners, and even animals have the chance of being reborn a Hindu male in return for the proper conduct of life on earth today and the observance of puja or sacrifice to the gods. This attitude explains why Hinduism is reluctant to make converts (though certain sects will take in outsiders); to be a Hindu a man must be born one. The American who wants to undergo conversion to Hinduism is told that only by a good life will he have the chance of reincarnation as a Hindu.

The relative excellence of a new birth is determined by a man's karma, his fate in the light of his past actions, for good or evil. This is an unchangeable law of nature and works automatically, irrespective of God. "By good deeds a man becomes what is good, by evil deeds what is bad," says one of the Hindu scriptures. Because of this, one cannot commit an act of violence against any living thing. Not only can a man *not* kill another human being, he may not kill an animal either, or an insect. While this precept has not been followed literally throughout Indian history, it has cut down on the number of acts of violence, including war. The Jains, a heretical offshoot of Hinduism, go so far in practicing nonviolence that they cover their faces with a cloth so they won't breathe insects and kill them; many Jains will not go out at night for fear of stepping on some living creature. On the other hand, I have met a very strict Jain who runs a hotel where meat is served; he will not enter the kitchen on the theory that what he does not see does not exist. A strict Hindu will not kill bees in order to get the honey from a hive; he will wait patiently until it is empty, nor will he kill silkworms to obtain the cocoon.

There is a group of three other precepts which are also basic to the Hindu way of life. They are (in the common Hindu terms), dharma, artha and kama. Dharma is, roughly, duty or socially approved conduct—a man's relationship to his fellowman and to other living creatures. Religion as well as social custom and morality are included in dharma. Artha is success in the world, in business and politics. Kama is love—success in dealing with the other sex. In theory a man should follow the three precepts in a balanced manner. These same standards, in different words and phrases, are followed with varying emphasis in every culture and religion in the world: what gives them their special flavor in Hinduism is their pursuit in the light of rebirth, fate and nonviolence.

So far I have been describing the ordinary way for the ordinary man. This way is accompanied by a highly complex series of rites and rituals, prayers and charms, some of which touch upon the magical. Many of the prayers may be said only by Brahmans, who, if they are conscientious, are weighed down with an endless number of religious duties from the beginning of the day to the end. In many cases a person who is not a Brahman employs one to pray and per-

form the rites, as they would be profaned in the mouth and hands of a lower-caste supplicant.

Against this ordinary path there is an extraordinary one. Virtually any upper-caste Hindu may follow it if he wishes (and even Sudras and untouchables sometimes have an overwhelming call to be saints, for which they are honored and respected by others, even in the light of their caste). What is demanded is a complete and unstinting dedication to God. Some men, and a few women, may feel the call to this extraordinary path in childhood. They will be given to a guru or other holy man as a student, and will be raised in the ascetic way of life. Two of India's most recent popular saints, the nineteenth-century mystic Ramakrishna and the woman ascetic known as Anandamayi Ma, became sadhus, or holy people, in childhood. Two others, who were born in India and came to America to live, work and die, Paramahansa Yogananda (author of the famous *Autobiography of a Yogi)* and

Every fall, depending on the phases of the moon, Hindus, particularly Bengalis, celebrate Durga puja. (Durga is a form of the Great Goddess.) Statues are made of clay which are honored for three days and then immersed in a river, where they disintegrate. Here a priest in a rural community prays to an image of Durga. The woman in the sunglasses is a member of the family that "owns" the village.

Astrology plays a dominant role in Hindu life. Astrological charts are drawn up at birth and from time to time people will have new readings made, particularly at important events, like marriages.

Meher Baba, whose cult is very strong in the States, also began as child ascetics. More often the ascetic way is followed by older men and women whose children have grown up. The men become sannyasin or bhikkhus, wandering monks or hermits who live by begging or on alms; women are likely to join an ashram, or religious house. Such a holy person is beyond caste. To him or her all men and women are brothers and sisters. This way of life has been the ideal for millions of Hindus, as it was for Buddha and unknown numbers of other ascetics. It is still common today, without anyone being the least surprised.

That which is, is One. Sages describe it in manifold ways.

The ignorant say that love and God are different; none know that love and God are the same. When they know that love and God are the same they rest in God's love.

Day after day, O lord of my life, shall I stand before you face to face. With folded hands, O lord of all worlds, I stand before you face to face. Under your great sky, in solitude and silence, with humble heart, I stand before you face to face.

And when my work is done in this world, O King of kings, alone and speechless I will stand before you face to face.

He is the unseen seer, the unheard hearer, the unthought thinker, the understood understander. There is no other seer, no other hearer, no other thinker, no other understander. He is your Atman, the Inner Ruler, the Immortal.

All Hinduism is a constant search for God, for God the All-Powerful Being, for God expressed in His three million (or thirty-three million) aspects and incarnations. This profusion of "gods" has always been to the Westerner a sign of the "paganism" of Hinduism. Yet the reason is simple. Man is incapable of grasping God in a single form, so great is His power and glory. In the magnificent eleventh chapter of the Bhagavad Gita, the second-century B.C. book which is the best known in Indian literature, we see the blinding vision of God in His universal form. God, who has appeared on earth as Krishna, an epic warrior, drops his mundane aspect and reveals His Supreme Being, "possessing numerous mouths and eyes, glittering with divine ornaments, displaying divine signs, divinely garlanded, divinely

Shiva is one of the two great popular gods of Hinduism. He is usually seen with a female consort, here Uma. In any case, his companion is a form of the Great Goddess. Shiva is the destroyer, the fearful and the auspicious god, the Lord of Tears, the Lord of Knowledge, the Divinity of Time, the Giver of Joy, the Lord of Yoga, and a hundred aspects of life.

scented, all-shaped, all powerful, transcendent and limitless." In this effort to delineate God in all His glory for finite man, we see Him brighter than a thousand suns: "the entire universe is lodged as one being within the body of the God of gods." From this vision, Krishna's companion, the mortal man Arjuna, who serves as a kind of foil for the Divine Revelation, perceives God as the Universal Form. He sees God without limit —infinite of arms, eyes, mouths and bellies. "I see and I find no end, no middle, no beginning . . . the guardian of eternal law, life's Soul undying, birthless, deathless, yours is the strength titanic. Million-armed, the sun and the moon your eyeballs, fiery-faced, you blast the world to ashes." Prostrate before the thousand-membered Universal Being, Arjuna begs forgiveness and asks Krishna, God, to resume His earthly shape.

While the monotheistic religions like Judaism, Christianity and Islam see God in the shape of man, Hinduism perceives Him in all shapes. In another part of the Gita, Krishna, who is God, says: "Those who worship other gods of whom they are the devotees, it is but myself they worship."

While God Himself is the Divine Ground of Being, not all men can approach Him directly. Thus many Hindus, if not most, search Him out in the form of a lesser god, as one of His many aspects, or even in the form of an animal such as a snake or an elephant. These "personal" gods are known as ishwara

Shiva sometimes appears as Nataraja, the Cosmic Dancer. It was from Shiva's drums, during the great dance through which the universe was shaped, that the four forms of science arose. Thus, from Shiva comes Yoga, Vedanta (the study of metaphysics), Language and Music.

devi or isht dev, the personal god one worships. These ishwara devi create a problem for the outsider who is unable to understand their role in the magnificent vision that is Hinduism. The more educated and sophisticated Hindus find them difficult to explain, and it is true that many ishwara devi function purely on a superstitious level, particularly among the very simple and the poor.

Yet Hindus will say over and over, "God is one and infinite, the light of light," descending in different forms at different places according to time and circumstances. This multiplicity, rather than demeaning the concept of God, expresses His power, His munificence, His glory, His transcendence. "When I think of God, I don't think only of Kali or Lakshmi," a young Bengali Hindu told me. "The thirty-three million gods are just manifestations of God. We have a lot of rituals, a lot of superstitions—one's vision of God depends on one's literacy, but nobody looks upon these gods as pagan. We each approach God within the limits of our competence."

These lesser manifestations have their special, comprehensible characteristics which attract the worshipper. Shiva, to take but a single example, is both the god of destruction and the god of regeneration. He is both the god of ascetics and of certain sexual cults. He has a wife and two children. His wife is known variously as Kali, Parvati, Durga, Sakti, Devi and Uma (and so forth). One of Shiva's sons is Ganesh (or Ganpatti), the popular elephant god; the other, who is

A Hindu monk, called simply Dr. Brahmachari (the name means monk), visits members of one of his congregations in the Muslim area of Bengal. Dr. Brahmachari cares for about a dozen scattered Hindu communities. The words on the post mean "Listen to the Name [of God]."

virtually ignored, is Kartikeya, the god of war. Shiva has a large number of followers, called Shivaites (there are six major Shiva cults in all), who follow the path of jnana, or knowledge. An even greater number of Hindus prefer the path of bhakti, or devotion, followed by the devotees of the god Vishnu (who has been incarnated as Krishna and eight other gods). Shiva is also worshipped in the form of a stone, the lingam, the life-giving force, a cult that antedates the Aryan Vedic period.

Yet all of us are bound by our own cultural and intellectual conditioning in writing about God and in trying to define Him. I have been speaking of God in the masculine–He, His, Him. God appears in masculine forms in Hinduism, but also as neuter and, above all, in the Supreme form, Shakti, as feminine. The Cosmic Being has two aspects: male, which is inactive, and female, active. The female principle, Shakti, manifests herself in the form of the Mahadevi, the Great Goddess, who takes a multitude of aspects, benign, creative, playful, loving, terrible, destructive, and so on. The most popular and all-pervading form of the Mahadevi is Kali, the great black goddess whose cult is found all over India. Westerners have come to believe that Kali is the goddess of destruction, and out of this has come a frightful vision of the negative aspect of the Hindu soul. But this is a sorrowful distortion and there is another side. "We see Kali as the great loving Mother," a devout Hindu woman said to me recently in Calcutta. "I pray

Vishnu is god of the ocean and of the luminous sky. He is also a solar deity and protector and sustainer of the world. He is believed to undergo ten incarnations or avatars in order to save the world. His first was as a fish, as we see in this drawing. The tenth is still to come.

At Calcutta's famous shrine, the Kalighat, where a piece of the goddess Kali is believed to have fallen from heaven, a yogi sits in meditation. He is praying for world peace.

to Her as Mother." A yogi told me:
"What Kali kills is sin—hate, anger, lust
and so on. Kali kills in order to create."
A sixth-century hymn, the Kali Sutra,
speaks of Her as "Kali with the full
breasts," with which she nourishes the
world, and addresses her, "O Mother,
who gave birth to the world as its pro-
tectress." A commentator on the hymn
points out that "It is commonly said that
she destroys but that is not so. The goddess does not destroy. Man does. She
takes back what she has put forth." Kali
is earth, fire, air, water, ether—the five
"elements." She is also Mind, the Soul
(atman), the Supreme. She is the "Moth
(atman), the Supreme. She is the "Mother
of the whole universe." At the same time
this divine energy, Shakti, in a form other
than Kali, is Kundalini, the coiled. Kundalini is the serpent power hidden deep
in man, which when unleashed, ascends
in him to be united with the Divine.

One form of worship is known as jalsain, which involves sitting in meditation upon a bamboo platform over the water during the coldest part of the winter. The ascetic sits day and night engrossed in prayer and meditation, despite cold and hunger.

While Hinduism might be said to be
primarily a religion of the Spirit, it has
an extensive sacred literature, the most
extensive of any religion, which serves
as the vehicle of teaching and belief.
There are two types: shruti, which have
been handed down by God Himself, and
smirti, which come later and have divine
origin but have been transmitted through
man. The great texts of the ancient past,
the Vedas, are shruti. And when a Hindu
says the texts are divine, he means just
that. The Vedas first began to appear
about 2000 B.C. and were solely the

province of the Brahmans, the priests. They were initially handed down orally but were eventually committed to writing. They are vast in number and of the utmost sanctity, being, in the words of a contemporary Hindu, "nothing less than the Divine Truth itself, the inexpressible truth of which the Vedic texts are of necessity but a pale reflection. . . . The Vedas are infinite and eternal. They are that perfect knowledge which is God." More than any other sacred texts in the world, they claim to be divine in a special way. "God created the whole universe out of the knowledge of the Vedas." This means that "Vedic knowledge existed even before the creation of mankind. They themselves are authority, being the knowledge of God."

In a more prosaic definition, the Vedas are collections (there are four) of prayers, sacred formulae and rites, and charms and magic. They also contain astrological and medical knowledge. But what had begun simply and directly in the Vedas as the desire to reach God, became in the hands of the Brahman priests almost meaningless ritual, in which the precise act, the correct intonation of a prayer, the perfect gesture in a ritual were more important—and more "holy"—than the spirit. By the sixth century B.C., when Gautama Buddha was born, new currents were moving. Buddha, as a wandering ascetic in the great tradition, rejected the rigidity of Hinduism, and even more, rejected the Hindu idea of God, which was undergoing a kind of popular reaction by becoming warmer, more personal, more mystical than the Vedic ideal. About this time the smirti texts— God speaking through man—began to appear. These works include the Upanishads, a series of spiritual treatises of varying lengths in the form of verses, prayers, discourses, dialogues and instruction. (In all they total about the same length as the Bible.) But the greatest work of this period is the Mahabharata, a great epic poem three and a half times as long as the Bible. An account of the wars of ancient Indian kings, it tells various didactic and moral stories and incorporates a number of theological and philosophical doctrines. Set within the Mahabharata is a later work, the Bhagavad Gita (the Song of God), composed somewhere between 500 and 200 B.C. The Gita, which takes the form of an account of a battle between opposing factions of a princely family, is actually the story of the spiritual struggle of a great soul. Though most of the narrative takes place on the battlefield, it is concerned mainly with the vision of God in all things and of all things in God. In the Gita, God appears as the Lord Krishna, who serves as the charioteer of a man named Arjuna fighting to help his family regain their kingdom. The Gita is set against a new background: The long-lived Vedic period had been Brahmanic, priestly, with emphasis on sacrifice; now in the Gita the focus is on the theme of duty, and the chief protagonists are the men of the second caste, the Kshatriyas, or warriors.

The Bhagavad Gita is spiritually important for several reasons, one being that it lays the groundwork for a great religious lay movement, the cult of Krishna. He is identical with Vishnu, the god of the ocean and of the luminous sky, a solar and cosmic deity, the protector and sustainer of the world. It is also the first full statement of bhakti, a term which may generally be translated as devotion. Bhakti was a new current in the great river of Hinduism, leading man to God not through knowledge as in the Vedic past, but through love, piety, intimate communion with and surrender to a Divine Person, the Lord alone. The Lord is conceived of as a personal, all-powerful, all-merciful Being, both transcendent and immanent. He is Love and Infinite Beauty. One of the most important developments in Indian life, bhakti surpasses all others in its immediate appeal to the masses of people. The bhakti movement continued to develop, deepening and widening, with great spiritual works, saints and mystics. One of the greatest bhakti works, next to the Bhagavad Gita, is the Bhagavata Purana, which was written about the tenth century A.D. It is a long poem of eighteen thousand couplets, with religious disquisitions, stories, expositions and lofty doctrinal statements. It is a work full of warmly sensuous symbolism, reminiscent of the Song of Songs or the poems of Saint John of the Cross. Throughout, God in his merciful loving kindness is called upon to work in the hearts of the men and women who follow Him in the path of bhakti.

The saints are in my heart, but I am in the hearts of the saints; Anything but myself is unknown to them; Nor do I know anything at all but them.

The Hindu is a man alone with God. Hindu worship is basically an individual act, though at times groups of people may seem to be doing the same thing, and there are certain occasions where members of a family will join together in prayer, such as at a funeral pyre or a rite of commemoration. But there is no such ritual as communal worship on a periodic basis, as is found in Judaism or Christianity. When Hindus pray, as they do often, they are praying as individuals, though there may be hundreds or thousands together.

The higher a man's caste, the more he is bound to follow the traditional rituals. The Brahman, particularly, is likely to adhere to as much of the ancient rites as time allows today. If he lives in a village or town (80 percent of India's six hundred million people still live in the countryside), he will get up before sunrise and go to the nearest river or stream or pond to wash and bathe. Prayers and offerings are made during the day in the household shrine, or in shrines and temples dedicated to certain gods and goddesses. Each caste or subcaste is likely to have its own rites and prayers, which are exclusive. Most often in a family only one person will pray, on behalf of the others.

Rivers are central points of worship.

Women usually enter the rivers to bathe and pray apart from the men. They bathe completely clothed, say their prayers, then change to dry saris. The woman (bottom left) has cropped her hair as a sign of mourning.

If running water is not available, a man will say his pre-dawn prayers in a pond or a water tank or at the edge of the ocean. But the ideal is running water, and rivers are worshipped as sacred. The common Indian word tirtha, which now means "a place of pilgrimage," once denoted only "a bathing place on a riverbank." But the sacredness of rivers has never been fully or properly explained. Rivers were always sacred, and people migrated to them to take advantage of their known holiness. The cult of the river is one of the oldest in India. The proper adoration of a sacred river is a great pilgrimage, up one bank and down the other, from mouth to source and back.

The Ganges is the most sacred of all rivers. Hindus call her Ma Ganga, Mother Ganges, because she too is a life-giving power. A legend says that the Ganges drops from heaven, her fall cushioned by Shiva's long locks, into a cave in the Himalayas, and from there in a rapid descent of some thirteen thousand feet through the mountains to Hardwar, one of the seven sacred cities. At Hardwar the Ganges is joined by four other rivers coming up from the bowels of the earth. The Ganges is celebrated by a hundred and eight sacred names, which may be chanted like a litany (Resort of the Eminent, Sin-destroying, Creator of Happiness, Staircase to Heaven, Embodiment of the Supreme Spirit, are a few). She crosses India, on her way to the Bay of Bengal, where she breaks up into a number of "mouths," some in

Left. A Bombay office
worker, on his lunch
hour, prays at the
breakwater at the
harbour.

Right. The Sikhs are an
offshoot of Hinduism.
They emerged in the
sixteenth century in an
attempt to find a middle
ground between
Hinduism and Islam.
Though a minority in
India, they now
form one of the most
powerful religious,
political and cultural
forces in the country.
This is a Sikh sadhu,
with the traditional
waterpot of the holy
man.

Bangladesh and others in India. The
Gangetic city of Benares stands with
Jerusalem, Rome, Mecca, Constantinople
and Moscow as one of the great sacred
centers. Benares is dedicated to Shiva,
not to him as a person but as an aspect
of Brahma, the Supreme Power who in-
cludes everything and excludes nothing.
The sanctity of Benares is most manifest
at dawn, when the life-giving Sun appears on the horizon. The city is situated
on the north bank of the Ganges, but
because the river bends at this point,
Benares is geographically west. It is a
moving, deeply spiritual moment to
stand on the ghats, the stone steps lead-

ing down to the water, and to witness the sun bursting forth on the far horizon. Hinduism commands mankind to pray to the Sun, not out of idolatry but because the Sun is the foremost physical manifestation of the Divine creative power. Without the Sun, Hinduism says, man would not have existed. The whole of his being is Sun-born, Sun-produced, Sun-supported. All growing things depend on the Sun, and when a man dies, his body goes up in fire, the localized symbol of the Sun. So at dawn, and throughout the day, the devout Hindu, who may have traveled from the farthest point of India for this sacred act, stands in the holy waters of the Ganges and prays to God through the Sun, being washed at the same time by the gently flowing symbol of His love and grace, the river.

It is the tradition for women to have their hands decorated at the time of marriage. The work is done in wax and lasts for several days before wearing away.

At Hardwar, or Benares, or any of the other favorite places for prayer along the river, the Hindu meditates. Except for those people who have been taken as a student by a guru or yogi or other teacher, the average Indian learns his religion at home, primarily from his mother or other women in the family. Religion is a natural act: there is no separation of the sacred and profane. His work, his meals, his bathing, even his sex life, are sanctified by prayer, particularly if he is high caste. The supreme goal in life is a pilgrimage to Benares, and failing this, to whatever other holy city is convenient and within his capabilities. Many Hindus wait until old age before making the pilgrimage to Benares, in the event that they might die there. A number do, either worn out from the long trip and the round of shrines and temples that are visited, or from some innate psychological release, which tells them that one's sacred duties have been completed and now is the time to leave the body—the body, to the Hindu, being disposable—while the soul continues onward in the long journey of seeking release from the endless cycle of birth and rebirth. Some people will even retire to Benares in old age, to await death, living in small monasteries and convents, or as recluses along the edge of the river.

Each temple has a priest, or several. But the priest, a Brahman, will perform the ceremonies alone, without a congregation. If any people are present, they follow their own rites. Certain feast and festival days will bring out large numbers of worshippers. Generally speaking, a Hindu will worship wherever and whenever the spirit comes over him. He is obsessed with God, and what can be more natural than to adore God at that moment?

The passing Westerner turns his head in embarrassment. But a Hindu at prayer, standing at the edge of the sea, or on the steps of a tank, will attract a crowd, eager to observe the fidelity with which this man is praying.

Bestowing grace throughout one's life are the samskaras, a sacramental system (the root of the word is the same as the Latin), which parallels the Christian system. There are ten to forty samskaras, depending on how they are defined, for various stages in one's life, during pregnancy, at birth (in a kind of baptism), at the bestowing of the person's name, the first cutting of hair, initiation, and marriage, to list but a few. One of the most beautiful groups of samskaras comes at betrothal and marriage, taking different forms and rites among different castes. Normally the young people do not see each other until the day of the ceremony. Marriage is arranged by the respective families, since it is the families that are united, as much or more than the young couple. The central rite is beautiful and impressive. It is held before a fire, with certain foods being cast into it for symbolic purposes. Vows are taken in which the respective families pledge mutual love and aid. The climax

Two village men sit in a Bombay street during the days before a marriage ceremony. They sit for five days in silence, while around them their fellow villagers hold a rollicking festival to mark the coming marriages.

comes when the young people swear eternal love. The new wife leads her husband to a spot where they can see the North Star. She says: "Thou art steady, may I be steady in my husband's family." Her husband then says: "The sky is firm, the earth is firm, and this wife is firm in her husband's family." The wife: "I pay homage to you." The husband: "May you be long-lived." He adds: "I bind your heart and mine with the knot of truth. May your heart be mine. May my heart be yours." Most of the young couples live with the husband's family, and may well continue to do so into middle age, when the size of the joint family leads the older sons to break off and start their own households.

Since all life, in whatever form, is sacred, animals and lesser creatures partake in the Hindu reverence for what God has created. (There have been and still are Hindu soldiers, but usually these men belong to warrior castes. Fighting is their dharma, or duty, a role confronted and delineated in the Bhagavad Gita. There, Arjuna worries about whether or not he can fight a war and take life despite the prohibitions against it; the answer is that since it is his dharma, and he must follow it, he must fight and thus possibly kill.)

The cow is the supreme symbol of the Hindu reverence for life. Hindus, with the exception of the very poor (and the outcasts) who are so desperate they will eat anything, and the very enlightened, who are hoping to prove they are free of superstition, never touch meat of any kind. Neither will they eat eggs, poultry, or fish. The cow occupies a special place in Hinduism as a symbol of the entire subhuman world. Mahatma Gandhi made a number of statements about the place of the cow: "Man through the cow is enjoined to realize his identity with all that lives. The cow is a poem of pity. One reads pity in the gentle animals. She is the 'Mother' to millions of Indian mankind. Protection of the cow means protection of the whole dumb creation of God." He also said: "To my mind the life of a lamb is no less precious than that of human beings. I hold that the more helpless the creature, the more entitled it is to protection by man from the cruelty of man."

Thus the cow is an expression of the brotherhood between man and beast, of man's identity with all that lives. The cow is referred to as "Gau Mata" (Cow Mother) and is treated with the same respect as one would treat his own mother. The cow is consequently the symbol of the divine motherhood, of life, of fecundity, abundance.

The long series of foreign invasions that began with the Moghuls (they were Muslims) in the twelfth century A.D. struck at the basic life force of Hinduism. The Moghuls, who were aggressive, rough, and visionary, converted hundreds of thousands of Hindus to Islam. The majority of them were people from the lowest castes, who had virtually nothing to gain by remaining Hindu, and were also attracted by Islam's egalitarian and mystical aspects. Islam abolished caste, and the Moghul armies offered the poor a chance to revenge themselves upon caste Hindus. In the sixteenth century India was invaded by Christians. The French and the Portuguese brought Catholicism, the Dutch and English, Protestantism. Again, the majority of the people to be converted were low caste and untouchable. Christianity retained remnants of the caste system, and even today Christians will not easily associate with or marry people of another caste, even though they are fellow Christians. But the flood of conversions soon died out, and though India today has more Catholics than Ireland, for example, converts are added slowly.

These challenges by Islam and Christianity eventually brought about a reaction. In the nineteenth century a number of Hindu reform movements arose, some searching for a revival of Hinduism through the Vedas, others trying to winnow out the pantheon of gods and goddesses to focus on God Himself. Christian and Western techniques of propagation were adopted, and the Bible, which had been often inserted into the Indian educational system as a matter of course by the British, was examined and used by some where adaptable, though others completely rejected it. Mahatma Gandhi was deeply influenced by the Sermon on the Mount in the development of his nonviolent campaign against the British. Hindu missionaries began to go abroad, and a small

A young Bengali boy celebrates the festival of Divali, one of the most popular of all holidays in India. Fireworks are set off, gifts exchanged and parties given. The usual complaint is that, like certain Western religious feasts, Divali costs too much.

number of Hindu religious and cultural centers were established, primarily in English-speaking countries. What is interesting in the 1970s is that Hindu centers, founded by Indians and continued by Americans, are flourishing in the United States, attracting many young people. In the past their major appeal was to much older, and one might say, more lonely people.

But Hinduism is faced with a crisis. While village Hinduism might continue on the traditional level, it is in the cities, colleges and universities, in offices and factories that the challenges are being posed. An uncounted number of the younger generation are losing their faith in Hinduism, without finding an alternative. The challenge, as is obvious, comes from the technological age. It does no good for a staunch orthodox Hindu to claim that Indians invented the airplane aeons ago—"the Vedas say so"—when the very fact of the machine, any machine, forces changes in religious patterns. The factory and the office lead to a softening of caste, and this is a weakening of the very framework of Hinduism. The airplane, the tank, the automobile, the bus, the factory lathe, the tractor, the operating table, the typewriter, must be handled and serviced by whatever people can run them. Skill, not caste, is the deciding factor. Caste slowly erodes and with it the power of the Brahmans. The untouchable, who is not faced with the fear of caste pollution as a Brahman might be, has new opportunities before him. Democracy, the railway, the British system of law, the printing press, the radio, television, modern medicine, Marxism, all challenge traditional Hinduism. It took nineteen centuries for the Vedic religion to fuse with primordial Hinduism. But events in the twentieth century are measured in terms of seconds: a count-down for a rocket—or a nuclear explosion (India already has two atomic power plants)—runs from ten to zero. On the upper and outer margins among thinking, perceptive Hindus, beliefs are beginning to show signs of the strain.

Tradition says that mankind is in the sixth millennium of the Kaliyuga, the last of the four great stages of the world. This is the time of strife, sweat and toil. As the Kaliyuga progresses, evil will gather momentum and good will be completely annihilated. The redemption of the world will be achieved only by its destruction and reconstruction. To achieve this, Vishnu, the second member of the great Hindu trinity, will incarnate himself as Kalki, the destroyer, and bring about the end of the world either by a deluge or a fire. The Kaliyuga has barely begun, having started about the time of the founding of the great cities of the Indus valley. There are some four hundred and twenty five thousand years to the end, when the world will be reborn in a golden age. Then all men will be good, and evil will be absent from the earth. For the patient man, Hinduism is the best of all beliefs.

At Puri on the Bay of Bengal, a group of village women, who have come from miles around on foot or by bus, hold a celebration in honor of their ancestors. This type of worship is a very primitive form of Hinduism. The tray holds sliced fruit and flowers.

BUDDHISM

 When Ashoka, the great king of northern India who unified many of the Indian states into the first great Indian empire, swept across the dusty plains and into the forests and cities to hunt down and massacre his enemies on their farms and estates, in the humid jungles and even in the palaces and temples and hovels, he killed a hundred thousand people. Another fifty thousand more were sent away in chains into slavery, and in the dislocated times that followed this appalling massacre, another fifty thousand died of plague and starvation. As the emperor rode through the sprawling dead in his bloody war chariot, he looked upon his victims, saw the women weeping, their heads covered with their homespun rough white cotton, saw the black-faced children with hunger-swollen bellies, and was overwhelmed with remorse. "I have done wrong," he told the people of India. He had sought peace by war and had instead brought sorrow, devastation, and death. He called his generals and nobles together and announced that this had been the last war. From that day onward he said he would be a follower of the Lord Gautama

Buddha, a man of peace. From one end of his domains to the other, from the craggy mountains of Afghanistan to the tangled jungles of southern India, he erected a series of memorial pillars to announce that he, Ashoka, wanted to be a father to his people. Some of these pillars are still standing, and on them we can see his message of tolerance, reverence, compassion, truthfulness, sympathy and the sanctity of life of both man and animal.

Ashoka's reign marked the beginning of a great period of Indian culture and civilization. He sent his missions throughout the known world to preach the doctrines of Buddha, peacefully, quietly. One of his sons, Mahendra, is said to have converted forty thousand people in Ceylon, including the king. The king's daughter made a pilgrimage to India to obtain a branch of the sacred Bodhi tree under which Buddha had sat in meditation during his Enlightenment. Other missions went as far as Greece and Egypt. Buddhism spread peacefully, unlike Christianity which was sometimes carried by the sword, and eventually much of eastern Asia and the offshore islands became Buddhist in whole or in part. While Buddhists might wage war, wars were not fought in the name of Buddha.

We forget that Buddha was an Indian, the first great Indian and perhaps the greatest of all ages, not excepting Gandhi. His statues from no matter what

Buddha sits in the position of meditation, with one hand resting on the other. The shrine, a gift of a pilgrim, is at Bodh Gaya, where Buddha found enlightenment.

period do not portray him as a man we can get close to. His teachings are warm and human, though Westerners often find him cold and detached. But for most men he is the great compassionate Buddha who understands suffering as no other man has, and who found and taught the Middle Way, a way which avoids both Hell and Heaven. We cannot see him as the angry Moses, as the Suffering Christ or Christ Triumphant, or the irascible, tormented Muhammad, or even as a desert prophet, lean and hungry and buffeted by the wilderness. Buddha is the smiling, enigmatic man who has come to terms with life and death and has conquered both. "The Kingdom of Heaven is within you," says Jesus, but Buddha has already told the world that "Buddhahood [enlightenment] is in your heart, if you will only search."

When the West first began to study the East in the nineteenth century, European scholars came to the conclusion that the end of Buddhism is "Nothing," Nirvana. But is it? Is nothingness what a third of the world wants and strives for? Is inner peace gained at the price of (unnecessary) passivity? Perhaps we have been misled. Finding the Buddha within is hardly a passive act but a very positive one.

These huge footprints in stone, tradition says, are the Lord Buddha's. They are impressed at Bodh Gaya and are about twice the size of the average man's feet.

His name was originally Gautama, his family name Siddartha, from the clan of the Sakyas (consequently he is also called Sakyamuni, or the sage of the Sakyas). He was born in 563 B.C. and died in

483, plus or minus a few years, ancient records and oral tradition being what they are. He was a son of a small prince in northern India, whose kingdom lay at the foothills of the Himalayan mountains. The family, like most princes, were members of the warrior caste, the Kshatriyas, a fact that was to cause friction with the Brahmans, or Hindu priests, who resented the sanctity of someone who was born of a lower caste.

The story of Buddha's birth starts in a dim, legendary age, when a Hindu priest named Sumedha decided to become a "Buddha"—an enlightened one—in a future birth so that he would be able to preach the Truth to suffering mankind. During a period of meditation such as the average Hindu still might practice, Sumedha thought: "I am subject to birth, to decay, disease, to death. What would be proper would be for me to try to win the great, deathless state of Nirvana, which is tranquil and free from birth and decay, from sickness, sorrow and woe. Somewhere in the world is a road that leads to Nirvana and will release man from existence."

Following the traditional path of the Hindu who seeks the way to a life of holiness, Sumedha gave away his possessions and went into the forest to live as a hermit. Eventually another holy man, Dipankara (also known as a "Buddha" because he had already found enlightenment), passed through the forest. The local people had prepared a road for Dipankara, but there was a muddy patch in it. Sumedha lay down in it so that

Dipankara could pass without getting his feet dirty. Dipankara realized that this was the act of a very saintly man. With the powers he had attained as a Buddha he looked into the future and saw that Sumedha was destined to become a Buddha himself, the greatest of all Buddhas. He made a public statement saying so.

Later, alone in the forest, Sumedha went into meditation, examining the Ten Perfections necessary to Buddhahood, and decided he must follow them in his future births. Five hundred reincarnations went by. (The reader separates fantasy and legend from "fact" at his own peril; what the Westerner might accept in his own tradition he dismisses in others.) By now, Sumedha, who was then in the Heaven of Delight, realized that the time had come at last for him to be reborn for the final time. The Great Enlightenment was at hand. The gods and goddesses of the ten thousand world systems surrounded him to emphasize that this was indeed the time. Thoughtfully Sumedha considered the continent, the district, the tribe, and most important, the mother. At last he chose a small kingdom in northern India. The family were Kshatriyas, and the mother, the wife of the reigning prince, King Suddhodana of the clan of the Sakyas, was Queen Maha Maya.

Maha Maya had a dream in which she was carried off to the Himalayas, where she bathed in a lake and lay down to rest. An elephant appeared from the north, carrying a white lotus flower in

A Tibetan monk in exile in India. When the Chinese invaded Tibet, tens of thousands of monks fled to India, along with hundreds of thousands of lay people. Tibet had the highest concentration of monks, or lamas, in the Buddhist world.

his trunk; he seemed to touch her side and to enter her womb. When Maha Maya awoke, she told the dream to the court priests, who interpreted the dream as a sign that she had conceived a man child who would either become a Universal Monarch or a Buddha. I should add that at the moment of the incarnation, signs appeared in the heavens and on earth, the dumb spoke, the lame walked, men began to speak kindly to each other, musical instruments sounded, every tree put forth flowers and the earth was covered with lotuses, and lotuses floated down from heaven.

Maha Maya delivered the child during a walk in a park of sal trees. Four angels received him in a golden net, singing, "Behold, O Lady, rejoice, a great son is born to thee!" The child stood up, took seven steps and cried, "I am supreme in the world. This is my last incarnation. There will be no more births for me!"

Five days after the child was born the family held the traditional Hindu name ceremony, giving him the name Siddartha. Among the guests were eight soothsayers, seven of whom predicted that the child Siddartha would become either a Universal Monarch or a Buddha, but the eighth said with certainty that he would become a Buddha and nothing else. "What would the signs be that Siddartha would become a Buddha?" asked the king, being highly displeased at the prediction. "The Four Signs are as follows: a man worn out by age, a sick man, a dead man, and a hermit." The king decided that his son would never see such signs, and did everything possible to protect him. Siddartha was raised as a young prince, surrounded with luxuries and attendants, and was educated in both writing and the arts of war and peace. He excelled in all his studies, being particularly proficient as a warrior. To keep his son entertained, the king gave him an endless number of nubile girls. At sixteen it was decided to get Siddartha married. The final choice, after a display of Sakya maidens, was Siddartha's cousin Yasodhara, whom he particularly liked. The young couple were given three different palaces, for the three seasons of India. The ceremony was celebrated with great pomp. Yet, as Siddartha sat and watched the dancing girls, the cosmic Buddhas of the heavens made him hear the message to "Recollect your vow to save all living things. The time is at hand: this alone is the purpose of your birth."

Soon the Four Signs confirming his divine mission were revealed, despite the king's efforts to keep them from Siddartha. One day, Siddartha wanted to visit the royal gardens. The king ordered the city swept clean and everyone but the young and handsome banned from the street. But the gods intervened. As Siddartha was being driven in his chariot to the gardens, one of the gods appeared on the street in the form of an old man.

"What kind of man is this?" Siddartha asked the charioteer.

"An old man, weighed down by the years."

"Is this what happens to every man?"

The charioteer admitted that it was.

"Must all men, or this man only, yield to age?"

"This is the law of nature," said the driver. "It happens to everyone—men, women and children."

Sadly Siddartha returned to the palace. The king ordered more amusements to divert his son's mind. But a few days later, on another trip from the palace, he saw a sick man, and after that a dead man. "So this is life," said Siddartha. The fourth trip came soon afterward. Siddartha saw a beggar monk passing by in a yellow robe, looking serene and self-possessed. "Who is this man who is so serene?" asked Siddartha.

"A holy man, a bhikkhu, who has no desires and leads a life of austerity."

"Good. He is a happy man. Such a man is praised by the wise. I would like to be like him. His way will be my refuge and the refuge of others and will yield the fruit of life and immortality." He returned to the palace in peace.

The king surrounded Siddartha's pleasure palace with triple walls, doubled the guards and sent in more dancing girls. At the same time Yasodhara was having a frightening dream: she saw herself naked and mutilated; the land was devastated by storms; the sun, the moon and the stars fell from the sky. When Yasodhara told Siddartha about the dream, he told her not to be fearful. "Such dreams come only to the good and not to the evil. The meaning of the dream is that I

Though Buddha was Indian, he is usually iconized in the nationality of each nation that adopted Buddhism. This gilded statue in a Bankok temple is a Thai version of the Lord Buddha.

have completely fulfilled the way of wisdom. Everyone who has faith in me will be saved from the three evils, without exception."

It was time for Siddartha to seek the way to Buddhahood. Late that night he went to tell his father. The king was distraught: he ordered more guards, more girls, but the heavens mobilized too. The Four Kings of the Four Quarters and the thirty-three devas all had certain jobs to carry out. The forces of the world, and the force of the heavens, both good and bad, were poised against each other. As he was about to leave, Siddartha was told that Yasodhara had borne him a son. Siddartha went to see the boy, who was sleeping in his mother's arms, half-covered. Siddartha was afraid that if he awakened his wife, he would be prevented from leaving, so he went to the stable where his horse and chariot were waiting. The nature spirits lifted the horse ever so gently so his feet made no sound, the gates opened silently, the household staff, the guards and the dancing girls were all sleeping. As the last gate opened, Mara the Temptress appeared and told Siddartha that if he stopped there and returned, in seven days he would be made ruler of the Four Continents and all the islands. But Siddartha replied that he did not want to be sovereign of the world. "I will become a Buddha and make tens of thousands of worlds rejoice." And then he passed through the gates. He traveled a long way and crossed the Anoma River, where the chariot stopped. The driver,

Row upon row of Buddhas sitting in the lotus position of meditation reminds the average man that "Buddhahood is within"—that is, every man can be a Buddha too, if he so wishes. The figures form the decoration on the model of a stupa or shrine.

Channa, was told to return and inform the king about Siddartha's decision. Channa instead asked him to go back to his father and his people. Siddartha said:

"Even if I should return to my family because I loved them, in the end we would still be separated by death.

"The meeting and parting of living things is like clouds coming together and drifting apart, or like leaves falling from a tree. Everything in a union is only a dream."

Then Channa said he would stay and become a hermit too. But Siddartha took a sword, cut his long hair and threw it into the river. He took off the white robes he wore as a prince and put on the yellow of a hermit. The horse saw what had happened, licked his master's foot, and went off into the forest to die.

Siddartha remained in the forest a week in meditation, and then began his life as a wandering holy man, begging his food from village to village. A king recognized him and offered Siddartha his throne. He refused and went back into the forest to join a community of hermits. At this point the various biographies of Siddartha depart from the pure narrative, with its slightly unworldly charm, and discuss a series of important philosophical distinctions that had begun to occupy his mind. Up to now he had been acting in the tradition of the orthodox Hindu holy man, and outwardly he was to follow the role in many ways to the end of his life. But inwardly there were changes which led him away from traditional Hinduism. The first decision resulted from his living with the hermits. They endured painful practices of mortification of the body in order to attain a final happiness. What struck Siddartha was that there was no easy way of escape: men were suffering misery in order to be happy, and the happiness they were seeking, rightly understood, consisted of pain, which was always subject to the almost endless round of death and rebirth. He decided that these hermits, while following a commendable path, still allowed themselves to be imprisoned in an unbreakable cycle. The obvious answer was to find a state where nothing needs to be repeated. Since it is the mind that controls the body, it is thought that had to be controlled first. He said:

Neither purity of food nor the waters of a sacred river can cleanse the heart; water is but water, but the true place of pilgrimage is the virtue of a virtuous man.

He went to another hermitage and placed himself under the tutelage of a master named Alara Kamala, learning the degrees of ecstatic meditation step by step. Again there was an interior conflict. Alara taught:

The soul escaping from the body, like a bird from a cage, is declared to be free: this is the Supreme Brahman [Sacred Power], constant, eternal, without distinctive signs, which the wise who know reality declare to be liberation.

Siddartha found this dualistic terminology of soul and body unsatisfactory. He saw that a liberated soul was still a soul, and whatever condition it attains, it still must be subject to rebirth.

Since each successive renunciation is held to be still accompanied by qualities, I maintain that the absolute attainment of our end is only to be found in the abandonment of everything.

Everything.

He left the hermitage and went deeper into the forest. Five wandering holy beggars found him and followed him, expecting that he would show them the way to enlightenment. Now came a long period of trial, in which, in his efforts to break through the earthly barriers to enlightenment, Siddartha practiced an extreme mortification of his body, ending in a fast during which he is said to have eaten a single seed or a single grain of rice each day as the way to conquer birth and death. He said later:

"Just like a row of reed-knots my backbone stood out through the lack of food. Just as the rafters of a tottering house fall this way and that, so did my ribs. Just as in a deep, deep well you can see the sparkling of the water, so could you see my eyes sunk in their sockets. My head was shriveled and shrunk like an unripe gourd cut from the stalk and left to wither in the sun and wind." His body was a skeleton tied together with skin taut as a tent. One day he fainted.

The gods informed his father that his son was dead. But the king replied, "I can't believe it. My son would not die without attaining enlightenment." Siddartha recovered and the gods brought the good news to the king.

But this was another turning point. Mortification and fasting had not shown him the way. He told his companions that he was going to become a wandering beggar again—they left him, on the theory that he had failed himself and them, not having found enlightenment after six years of austerity, and went off to Benares—and now Siddartha became an ordinary holy man, eating ordinary food and begging and living just like any other holy man in India.

The account now takes a new turn. Living nearby Siddartha's forest hermitage was a young woman named Uruvela, the daughter of a local herdsman. Uruvela had the practice of feeding eight hundred Brahman hermits and wandering monks every day. An angel appeared to her in a dream and told her that the Bodhisattva (the term means "one who is on the way to Enlightenment," that is, Buddhahood) had ended his fast and was to be fed. So Uruvela brought an offering of boiled rice and milk to Siddartha, who was sitting under a great tree in the jungle. Siddartha divided the food into forty-nine portions and took the bowl to the edge of the river. He put it in the water, saying to himself that if he was to receive enlightenment that day, the bowl would go upstream. It swiftly floated away against the current and disappeared upriver. Siddartha sat in contemplation for a while at the river's edge and then returned to the great tree, where he was to endure a dark, anguished day, tormented and buffeted by Mara the Fiend, by hosts of devils and demons, by frightful storms, by showers of rocks and burning ashes, and then by the temptations of beautiful women—a long list of horrors and temptations such as many holy men of all faiths have been said to experience on the threshold of enlightenment.

At last the onslaught ended. Before the sun had set, Siddartha's victory over the forces of evil had been won. Then

Though Buddhism generally avoids extremes, such as fasting and penances, some Buddhists, among them the Tibetans, do practice certain forms of mortification of the flesh. Some monks and pilgrims, like this man, will raise and prostrate themselves by the hour in atonement for their sins.

The great monastic complex at Sarnath, founded upon the place where Buddha preached his first sermon, has fallen into ruins with the decline of Buddhism in India. It is now being excavated and restored by the Indian government.

Siddartha, now becoming the Buddha, the Enlightened Being, sank deeper and deeper into meditation. As night fell, he reached the Knowledge of the Former States of Being, then the Omniscient Vision, followed by comprehension of the Chain of Causation which is the Origin of Evil. Before the sun rose again, Siddartha attained Perfect Enlightenment. At this great moment, say the ancient Buddhist texts, innumerable wonders were manifest. One commentator says: "The earth quaked six times, and the whole universe was illumined by the supernatural splendour of the sixfold rays that proceed from the body of the seated Buddha. Men's hearts experienced a flowing of love, the sick were healed and all creatures found peace and rest."

Siddartha Gautama is now the Buddha, the Enlightened One. From now on he will be called that, though he himself never uses the term. He sits for seven days, motionless in the bliss of Nirvana. Upon arising he stands for another seven days, lost in the contemplation of the spot where he had won the fruits of the countless deeds of heroic virtues gained in five hundred incarnations since he first became aware of the desire for Enlightenment. Buddha then spends another seven days walking back and forth along a cloistered path. After this comes seven days seated in a pavilion made by the gods, contemplating the teachings of the Abhidhamma Pitak, book by

book; at the same time he meditates on the doctrine of causality. He has seven days of sitting again under the tree where Uruvela left him the milk and rice, and seven days under the hood of the snake king, Mucalinda, while a storm rages. And finally he sits for seven days beneath a rajayatan tree enjoying the sweetness of liberation.

Thus, forty-nine days pass. The Buddha has no bodily wants but lives on the joy of contemplation, the joy of the Eightfold Path and the joy of its fruits, Nirvana. Then he bathes and eats. Two Brahmans come along and offer him honey cakes and rice, and become his disciples.

Reflecting on the depths of the Truth he has discovered, Buddha wonders if it would ever be possible to communicate it to others. But the goddesses quickly come and say, "The world will be lost," and persuade him to proclaim the Truth to all mankind. But to whom should he reveal the truth? The answer comes: to the five disciples who had rejected him. He finds them outside Benares, the most holy of India's seven holy cities. In the Deer Park at Sarnath, five miles from Benares, he preaches to them. This is his first sermon, which is called "Setting in Motion the Wheel of the Law, or the Foundation of the Kingdom of Righteousness." Buddha speaks:

There are two extremes to be avoided.

On the one hand, habitual devotion to the passions, to the pleasures of sensual things (which are ignoble and

Under the Bodhi Tree—the Tree of Enlightenment—is where Buddha sat during his interior search. A cutting from the original tree was brought to Ceylon. Since the first tree had in the meantime died, a cutting was returned to Bodh Gaya. This, in effect, is the Tree in its third generation.

Buddha, with companions, in a very Indian-like pose: seated on a lotus throne, in the lotus posture, with the hands in the gesture of peace.

unprofitable). On the other, habitual devotion to self-mortification (which is also painful, unprofitable and ignoble).

There is a Middle Path, a Path which opens the eyes and leads to understanding, which leads to peace, to insight, to the higher wisdom, to Nirvana.

This is the Noble Eightfold Path, that is to say, Right Views, Right Aspirations, Right Speech, Right Conduct, Right Mode of Livelihood, Right Effort, Right Mindfulness, and Right Rapture.

There is suffering, and the noble truth of suffering is this: birth is painful, old age is painful, disease is painful, death is painful.

Contact with the unpleasant, separation from the pleasant are painful.

The origin of suffering comes from both the burning thirst and the desire for sensual pleasures, and the craving for material success.

The Noble Truth to eliminate pain is this: to conquer passion, to give up, to get rid of, to be emancipated from, this burning thirst.

The Noble Truth of the Eightfold Path leads to the ending of pain.

During the next five days, the five monks, each on a different day, attained Enlightenment. On the fifth day, Buddha called them together to give a sermon, "On the Nonexistence of the Soul."

The body cannot be the eternal soul, because it will be destroyed. Nor can the eternal soul be sensation, perception, the predispositions, consciousness, because they too will pass.

Is form permanent or transitory? Are sensation, perception, predispositions and consciousness permanent or transitory?
The disciples answer: "Transitory."
And is the transitory good or evil?
"Evil," say the disciples.

And this evil which is so transitory, can you say that this is mine, this is "I," this is my eternal soul?
The disciples say, "No."
Then it must be said that all physical form, past, present, future, subjective or objective, far or near, high or low, is not mine, not I, not my eternal soul.
Knowing this, the true disciple will reject physical form, sensation, perception, predisposition and consciousness, and will be freed of desire, and will be aware that he is free, and he knows that

A stylized Buddha in black stone. The small spot in the center of the forehead, sometimes known as the Third Eye, indicates that he has passed beyond the limits of his earthly body.

*at the end of his life, he has lived the
pure life, he had done what is necessary,
and that he has put off mortality that is,
being reborn again for ever.*

Through this dialogue the minds of the
five disciples were completely enlightened, and the next day fifty-five more
disciples came and attained enlightenment, making sixty in all. The Buddha
sent them out to preach. Thirty young
princes came and attained enlightenment. The Buddha next disputed with
three Brahmans who were fire worshippers, and received them with their
disciples. This led to his third sermon,
the Discourse on Fire.

*All things are on fire.
What are these things that are on fire?
The eye is on fire,
Forms are on fire,
Eye-consciousness is on fire,
Impressions received by the eye are on
fire.
Whatever sensations—pleasant, unpleas-
ant or neutral—that originate in the eye
are likewise on fire.*

*And with what are they on fire?—with
the fire of lust, of resentment, with the
fire of glamour, with birth, old age,
death, sorrow, misery, grief and despair.
The ear, the nose, tongue, the sense of
touch are on fire.
The mind too, the thoughts are on fire.*

*All things are burning. The true monk
rejects these things that cause fire, and*

he thereby puts off birth and rebirth forever.

As the result of the Fire Sermon, a thousand disciples were freed from attachment, and delivered from the chains of desire, and attained Nirvana.

The life of Buddha followed the pattern of the wandering holy men of India, which even today is hardly changed. During the monsoon rains of the summer, Buddha and his followers kept "vassa," the rainy season, by staying with a prince or a wealthy man. When the rains had stopped, Buddha and his disciples would set out on foot to preach, walking from one village or town or city to another, followed by great groups of people, who would join for a few days and then drop out, to be replaced by others. He made no plans, but begged for food and shelter as he went. In the outskirts of a few large towns, monasteries were built by wealthy followers where he could stop to pray and meditate and to meet pilgrims. These monasteries had dormitories, houses, halls, cloisters, kitchens and storerooms. They were surrounded by mango and palm trees for shade, and often had pools and tanks with lotuses and fish. Kings, wise men, lay people, the rich and the poor, came to see him. And then, when he was rested, he would suddenly walk out of the monastery, followed by a group of disciples bearing his begging bowl and shawl. On the road he would arise before the sun ("The hours before dawn are the best for prayer and meditation," an Indian holy man told me recently) and spend his first waking minutes in contemplation; then he would talk to his disciples. When it seemed likely that the townspeople were awake, he would enter the town with his begging bowl, receiving food (or being rejected) with his eyes downcast. (The standard offering today to such begging monks is some rice, and occasionally vegetables such as lentils or greens, and sometimes yogurt.) However, Buddha would often receive an invitation from a king or a wealthy man to come to a meal. This meant that he delivered a sermon, and had a period of conversation and instruction, and sometimes a dispute with religious men who followed a different way, which Buddha tried to reconcile with the Truth as he had received it and taught it. It was a serene way of life. Buddha preached peace and Enlightenment, and the people responded.

We are what we think,
having become what we thought.
Like the wheel that follows the cart-pulling ox,
Sorrow follows an evil thought.

And joy follows a pure thought,
like a shadow faithfully trailing a man.
We are what we think,
having become what we thought.

Clear thinking leads to Nirvana,
a confused mind is a place of death.

The monk, usually called the bhikkhu, forms the core of Buddhism. After a lengthy period of instruction he goes through three stages of ordination before becoming a full member of the monastic community. Ordinarily he spends the first part of his day in obtaining food by begging or manual labor, and the afternoon in prayer, contemplation and study.

Clear thinkers do not die,
the confused can never live.

Planners make canals,
archers shoot arrows,
craftsmen fashion woodwork,
the wise man molds himself.

You are your own refuge;
there is no other refuge;
This refuge is hard to achieve.
One's self is the lord of oneself;
there is no other lord.
This lord is difficult to conquer.

Let us live happily,
hating none though others hate.
Let us live without hate among those who
hate.
Living with fools is endless pain.
Better to live with an enemy instead.
Living with wise men, like living with
kinsmen,
brings happiness.
Like the moon moving among star
clusters,
one should move among the wise,
the holy, the faithful, the noble—
this is the essence of wisdom.

Buddha's death came suddenly, in his eightieth year. He had visited the home of one of his disciples, where he was given a meal of rice, pork and sweet cakes. Many of the writings gloss over his eating of meat at this last meal, but apparently, though he would not kill an animal, he would eat the flesh if someone else killed it. He became ill with dysentery and cramps. He made a partial recovery, and set out on his journey again, accompanied by a favorite disciple named Ananda. At the edge of a stream he stopped, feeling weak. He sat down on his cloak and asked Ananda to bring him some water. A new disciple came along, with another cloak, made of finely spun gold, but when it was put on Buddha's shoulders, the gold paled, because the skin of an Enlightened One, especially on the day of his death, is brighter than gold. Buddha then went down to a river and bathed and drank, and then sat on the bank, talking to Ananda and the villagers who were coming to hear his last words. He stretched out on his side. His mind was clear, and he was self-possessed. His final words were ones of both negation and encouragement:

"Decay is inherent in all component things. Work out your salvation with diligence!"

I have dwelt for some time on the life of Gautama Buddha for a number of reasons, one being that in the West so little is known about him (what I have given here is but a fraction of what has been written). Also, there are certain elements in his life story which bring out the kind of legend and folklore that has encrusted Buddhism, much as its more intellectual practitioners would like to keep it "pure." Then there are certain elements in his life which he shares with holy men in other parts of the world.

I think we have to be tolerant to the legends and myths. They stem from an age when myth-making was part of the literary and religious heritage, and it is difficult to say how seriously they are taken—there are similar folk stories about Christ, which are completely fanciful and yet played an important role in the iconography of the Christian Middle Ages. However, they do not make Christ any less real, nor do the fanciful stories about Buddha make him any less real, either. A belief as widespread and as complex and as true in its humanity as Buddhism does not start with falsehoods or a conspiracy to fool the world. It begins with a person, a thought, an idea, a desire, a search, a true heart, and it grows in the hearts of millions of people who themselves are searching for a Way, a way that shows that Enlightenment is not without but within.

What Buddha shares besides the search, the retreat from the world while attaining Enlightenment, and the preaching to all mankind and not a select few, is the fact that he did appear on the historical scene at a definite point in time, after the world had been prepared for his coming, much as Christ's coming had been prepared by the prophets. Then there was that precise moment (at the age of twenty-nine in Buddha's case) when he decided to break with the ordinary and to fulfill his mission. He could build upon orthodox Hinduism, when necessary, but he was not afraid to challenge and break with it in the name of Truth. His mere presence was a confrontation with the established order. He denied the caste system, which both enlivens and enervates Hinduism, and he showed the way to all men, not to a minority as in Indian orthodoxy (the Brahmans), so that all may attain enlightenment too.

The "truth" of the "myth" of the life of Buddha cannot be approached in rational terms as we would in the West. Whether or not it is *literally* true is not the issue. What is relevant is the experience of the Buddha: the milieu, the reaction, the thinking-out, the suffering, the decision and renunciation and the self-imposed loss. I could have glossed over the legends, but they exist and are part of Buddhism, though many Buddhists are said to be ignorant of them, and others reject or are ashamed of them. What matters most, in the end, is *what* he taught.

Buddha was not born a "Buddha" but became one by his own efforts. What he did, what he taught, was within the possibilities of any human being. Buddha is not a saviour who gratuitously saves others via his own personal salvation or sacrifice. "To depend on others for salvation is negative," he said, "but to depend on oneself is positive." He did not claim the monopoly of Buddhahood, which he said was not the prerogative of any one person, no matter how specially graced. Buddhahood is freely available to every man. Men are not wicked by nature but by ignorance. At conception man is pure at heart; eventually the delusions of evil afflict him. Unseen—supernatural—powers do not condemn man, nor free him. Man gains his deliverance and purification by his own efforts without depending on an external god or on the intercession of priests.

The result of this teaching is that Buddhism is essentially a nonaggressive but deeply moral and philosophical system which finds the idea of God, or "God," or gods totally irrelevant. God does *not* exist in Buddhism, either as a supreme personal creator in the Judaeo–Christian–Islamic tradition, or as the Energizing Force in the multitudinous forms of Hinduism.

Buddhism demands no blind faith from man, has no dogmatic creeds, encourages no rites or rituals (though such do exist, and Buddhism is riddled with superstitions). What is taught is the golden mean, the Middle Way which guides its disciples through pure living and pure thinking into the attainment of supreme wisdom and deliverance from evil.

One of the most striking qualities of Buddhism is its practicality. It is not concerned with insoluble problems. The Way is available and open to every man if he wishes. There is no appeal to a higher power. Liberation is within. There are no sacraments, no secrets or mysteries. Buddha said: "Three things shine before the world and cannot be hidden. The sun, the moon, and the Truth proclaimed by the Thathagata [the fully

enlightened Being, that is himself]."
Hinduism, particularly from the time of
the Vedic age, was obsessed with
prayers, magical formulae and sacrifices.
Buddha saw that they were not essential
for deliverance. Misery and suffering
were not the result of angry gods who
must be propitiated but of man's ignorance and inability to develop fully.

Since there is no supernatural above
man, there is no supernatural within
him. I once asked a Singhalese monk
about God, the Creator, the Supreme
Being, the ground of All Being, remark-
ing that in my readings in Buddhism I
had never come across even a negative
mention of God. He was silent for a
moment and then said: "The Lord
Buddha was asked the same question
and he avoided an answer, saying that
God, that the question of a Creator, was
irrelevant." In essence, the question is
nonsensical. If God is perfect, the All-
Perfect Being, say Buddhists, how can
He create imperfection, the imperfect
man, the imperfect universe? I suspected
that my question made the monk uneasy
because the concept of a Supreme
Power is one that had never entered his
mind, not being one that Buddhists
dwell upon, even to dismiss. What is
important is kamma, dhamma and rebirth. Kamma (the Hindu word is karma)
means "action," but in its ultimate sense
it is "worthy and unworthy" act or will
—kamma constitutes both good and
evil: good begets good and evil begets

evil. What we are today is the result of
our past actions, in this life and in our

past life. Kamma is neither fate nor predestination. It is not something imposed upon us by another power but is the result of our own doing. In order to avoid the negative effects of kamma, one works toward a better kamma in this life and, above all, for the next.

As long as the kammic force exists, man is tied to kammic rebirth. At the moment of conception it is past kammic energy that conditions the initial consciousness of the foetus. It is this invisible kammic energy that vitalizes the phenomenon of life, both the body and the mind of the sentient being. What returns in each birth is kammic energy, there being no such thing as a "soul" in Buddhism. The energy accumulates for good or bad.

The unending chain of kammic rebirths is broken by nibbana (in Hinduism, Nirvana). The goal of every man is to break the kammic chain and to attain this final nibbana. Westerners take the word to denote a kind of passive state, but Buddhists say that nibbana is completely positive. The original Sanskrit phrase means nonattachment. Nibbana, as the Buddhist sees it, is not mere nothingness or annihilation. There is no precise translation or definition. one must experience it. The best one can say in explanation is that nibbana is a superworldly state of being. Though it may be obtained after death it can also be achieved in the present life.

In explanation Buddha said, "The Arahat [enlightened soul] who has been released from the five aggregates [cer-

In some Buddhist countries young men are expected to spend a fixed period of time, usually from six months to three years, as monks. After this period they may return to civil life. These are novice monks in Thailand.

tain psychological attributes] is deep, immeasurable like the ocean. To say he is reborn is not so, to say that he is neither reborn or not reborn is also not so."

The road to nibbana begins first of all with an understanding of basic Buddhist tenets, most of all, the Noble Eightfold Path. The Path culminates in Right Concentration. This leads to intense meditation, jhana (dhyana in Hinduism, ch'an in China, zen in Japan) which, successfully practiced, brings the spiritual pilgrim deep into samadhi. Meditation is open to anyone, but it is the special province of the celibate monk to practice it to the best advantage. Samadhi is "one-pointedness of mind," a state in which the mind has settled on a single subject for meditation, depending on one's temperament. This subject is explored internally. A simple physical goal such as breathing might be the first step; here the person in meditation tries to control and subdue the normal inflow and outflow of air. Next might come meditation upon one of the four sublime states: loving-kindness, compassion, sympathetic joy, or equanimity. Eventually one gains ecstatic concentration and becomes entrapped in jhana, enjoying the serenity and calmness of the one-pointed mind. At this stage the comtemplative is able to develop the Five Supernatural Powers—the Divine Eye, Divine Ear, Reminiscence of Past Births, Thought Reading, and Psychic Powers. However none of these is essential for Buddhahood, and the true seeker will not use the last two Powers except in

The Japanese tea ceremony is derived from a Zen practice
originally developed to keep Zen monks awake. It developed
into a comtemplative exercise, done with precise movements
and rhythm. Each gesture is a form of meditation.

the most sparing manner. All of these Powers are gifts, so to speak.

The final stage is insight, the ability to see things as they really are. The mind of the contemplative now resembles a "polished mirror." Wherever he looks he sees nothing but life's Three Characteristics—transience, sorrow and soul-lessness—outlined starkly. There are still Fetters to overcome, the Fetters of self-illusion, doubt, and indulgence in wrongful rites. If the seeker should die at this point he will return seven times more, but he already has such a lead that he will be spared the multitudinous rebirths required of most of mankind. Having overcome the Fetters there are still two more obstacles, sense desire and will. If these can be discarded, the seeker becomes an anaga-mai, a never-returner.

After death he is born again in the Pure Abodes. But the struggle is not yet finished. There are more Fetters to be broken—lust after earthly life, restlessness, and ignorance. Passing these obstacles, the seeker reaches the unutterable bliss of nibbana.

Buddha's teaching, given in the form of sermons, homilies, fables, parables, similes, and folklore, was adapted to the capabilities of each particular audience. He did not practice miracles (though some have been attributed to him) and he forbade his followers to use them. The only worthwhile miracle, he said, was when man was led by instruction to "the right use of his intellectual and ethical powers." Buddha left no written records, but his disciples, after his death —the year was probably 483 B.C.—met in a Great Council to establish his true teachings and to put them into writing. They assembled a vast collection of his works and sayings, the Tripitaka, or Three Baskets, which fall into three general categories: The Basket of Discipline, the Basket of Discourses, and the Basket of Ultimate Doctrine, each of which contains further divisions. The first contains conversations by Buddha, the second was established for his disciples, and the third consists of discussions by Buddha and his followers, with commentaries by various disciples. They were first put down in Pali, a vulgarization of Sanskrit, the classical Indian tongue, but since Buddha had urged his followers to learn his teachings in their own languages there is no "official" Buddhist language as Sanskrit is for Hindus, or Hebrew for Jews and Latin for Roman Catholics. The guiding principle of Buddhist doctrine is that whatever is rightly spoken and free from error is the teaching of Buddha. A Chinese Buddhist reformer, Lao-tzu, said, "The True unwritten word is always rotating. All heaven and earth are repeating words of truth. The true book is not outside of man's life. The dhamma that is invisible manifests itself spontaneously and needs no book." However, oral tradition, which is very accurate and reliable in the East, continued for some four hundred years. Buddha's teachings were propagated through most of the Eastern world during the next few centuries, partly through writings and sometimes verbally. There was even some influence upon the West. These teachings, or rather, various interpretations of them and the schools they inspired, fell into two main groups, each with several subdivisions. For general purposes they are the Hinayana (the Little Way, or the Little Raft) and the Mahayana (the Greater Way, or the Great Raft), which are also known as the Southern School and the Northern School, because they spread in these directions, Hinayana through southern India, Ceylon, Burma and southeast Asia, and Mahayana through northern India, Nepal, Tibet, China, Korea and Japan. Out of Mahayana Buddhism there came a minor school, Tantric Buddhism in Tibet and Mongolia, which contains a large amount of magical and occult beliefs and practices, and Zen Buddhism, which was very important in China, and which eventually became the dominant form in Japan. The differences between Hinayana Buddhism and Mahayana Buddhism (to simplify highly complex doctrines) are primarily these:

Hinayana Buddhism (the Little Vehicle) earned its name as a term of derision on the part of the more energetic Buddhists of the north, who saw Hinayana as not only too rigid in its orthodoxy, but at the same time amiable and serene in its self-centeredness. Hinayana aims at the salvation of the individual through knowledge. The Hinayana ideal is the arhat, the monk who seeks his own deliverance, the saint for his own sake, while the Mahayana ideal is the Bodhisattva, the man who tries to help others to their own way of salvation; it is a more altruistic path.

Self-salvation, the Hinayana way, is an exceedingly difficult Path, while Mahayana follows the Middle Way in a more relaxed manner, not demanding that a man should renounce the world immediately. It is, to explain both schools in the simplest manner, the way of knowledge versus the way of love and action. The man who is saved by knowledge stands apart from the world and its hopes and fears, offering his knowledge to others so they may stand apart also. The man who is moved by love and wisdom to activity offers others the same goal but with different means.

ZEN. Buddhism has long had an attraction for the Western world. Some of the Jewish sects of the Dead Sea, in the century before Christ, are believed to have been influenced by Buddhist ideals of monasticism. Later on, the Christian desert fathers, who retreated into the burning wastes of Egypt and Syria, were similarly influenced. The Church Fathers Clement of Alexandria, Origen, and Jerome all mentioned Buddha and his teachings. But the influence was subtle and not very direct, and underwent transformations not unlike the cycle of birth and rebirth. For example, the legend of Saint Josaphat, a very popular figure in Armenia and Middle Eastern nations, is basically a baptism of Buddha into Christian terms, Josaphat being a corruption of "Bodhisattva." The Jesuit missionaries who traveled to the Far East in the sixteenth and seventeenth centuries studied Buddhism, primarily as a way of finding the means by which Buddhists could be converted to Christianity. But in the early nineteenth century, Western scholars began true research into Buddhism and into Buddhist texts, and a number of "authoritative" but not very accurately translated versions of Buddhist works were made in various European tongues. Westerners had the understandable but regrettable practice of putting Buddhist texts into European and Christian terms and of becoming so involved in obscure points of grammar in Sanskrit, Pali, Tibetan and Chinese and other Asian languages that the basic doctrines of Buddhism were often obscured and lost. But in the long view of history a few centuries mean little. There is a Buddhist upsurge in the West, in the form of a kind of Buddhism —Zen—that some scholars say isn't even Buddhism. Zen has had a great flowering in America and Europe, spreading through the beat, flower, and hippie generations, aided by the speed and techniques of modern methods of communication. Zen in America has been presented in a variety of forms, on many levels. Jack Kerouac, one of the first spokesmen for the beat generation, spoke unendingly of Zen (*The Dharma Bums*, for example), and Alan Watts, once an Episcopalian minister, has written widely on Zen, in books that range

from simple statements to heavily complex works. A number of Westerners have spent long periods in Japanese Zen monasteries; one of the most knowledgeable of these is Philip Kapleau, whose masterful *Three Pillars of Zen* is one of the best works by a Westerner on this most demanding, most complex —yet most simple—form of Buddhism. The Roman Catholic monk Thomas Merton, who was drawn to Buddhism in the nineteen-thirties as a teenager in England, spent the last ten years of his life going further and further into Buddhism and then into Zen; he died in Asia during a search for Zen sources, having written of Zen with great understanding and feeling. "Do you approach the study of Zen with the idea that there is something to be gained by it?" asked Merton. "Where there is a lot of fuss about 'spirituality,' 'enlightenment,' or just 'turning on,' Zen enriches no one." He adds: "Zen is consciousness unstructured by particular form or particular system, a transcultural, transreligious, transformed consciousness."

In Zen one does not see Buddha, one *is* Buddha. A Zen master, Shen Hui, said, "The true seeing is where there is no seeing." Zen is outside all structures and forms. Another Zen master, Zenkei Shibayama, writes that Zen is a mirror, "thoroughly egoless and mindless. If a flower comes it reflects a flower, if a bird comes it reflects a bird. Everything is revealed as it is." But one cannot "study" Zen, the masters say over and over again. Zen has no definition. The way to study

The abbot of a lamasery in the Cauvery valley area of southern India welcomes guests.

Zen is to penetrate the outer shell and taste the inner kernel which cannot be defined. Thus one discovers reality. Reality is the core of Zen, but what it is and what it is not, is not to be labeled. This apparent evasiveness infuriates the logically minded man, but until logic is transcended we cannot "understand."

"What is the nature of Ultimate Reality?" asked a disciple.

The Buddha pointed to a vase of flowers.

"Not a word came out of his mouth," says one of the sacred books. "Nobody understood the meaning of this except the venerable Mahalasyapa, who quietly smiled at the Master, as if he fully comprehended the meaning of this silent but expressive lesson by the Enlightened One."

This is pure Zen teaching. It is a cliche to state that "it is impossible to define Zen in words," yet all the preliminary approaches to Zen have to be verbal. (I use the Japanese term, Zen, rather than the Indian, Dhyana, or the Chinese, Ch'an, or the Vietnamese, Thien, which are all less familiar.) Zen is nonverbal. It is expressed in a glance, a phrase, a silence, a blow, an action; when words are used, they are used in another context. ("What is the sound of one hand clapping?")

A monk asked Tosu, a Zen master: "Am I right when I understand that the Buddha asserts that all talk, however trivial or derogatory, belongs to Ultimate Truth?" Tosu said: "Yes, you are correct."

The monk then said: "Then may I call you a donkey."

Buddhist teaching is often done on a one-to-one basis, with the pupil sitting at his teacher's foot.

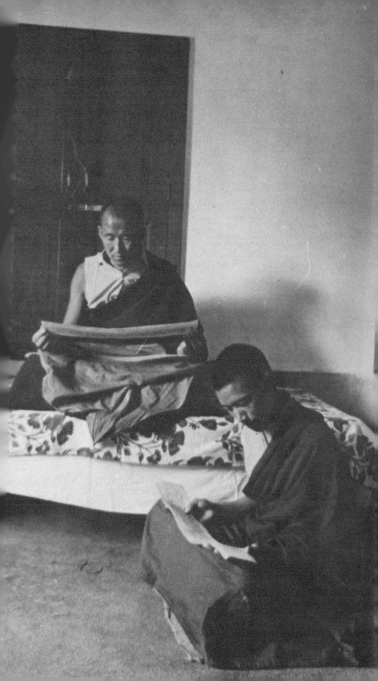

Tosu struck him.

Briefly, what happened was that the monk was being "logical," and letting his mind stay chained in pedantic thought. Tosu struck him, not out of anger but to force the monk to break his logical pattern of thought.

The reason for breaking thought patterns is to bring the monk to satori, or enlightenment. Yet the qualities which distinguish Zen from other types of Buddhism are hard to pinpoint. Zen is direct, natural, and even obvious. Awakening may occur at any moment, though the disciple may often spend years in preparation. What distinguishes Zen is its "flavor." (I don't think any other form of religion has ever been defined so much with this one word.) What gave Zen its first widespread form was its adoption by the Chinese in the sixth century when the first authenticated Zen master, Bodhidharma, arrived from India in A.D. 527. He was summoned by the Emperor Wu.

The emperor asked if he could acquire merit by building temples, distributing scriptures, and giving alms.

"Not at all," said Bodhidharma.

"What then does true merit consist of?"

"In the obliteration of matter through Absolute Knowledge, not by external acts."

The emperor apparently felt puzzled and frustrated, so he asked Bodhidharma if he knew whom he was standing before.

"No." Thereupon Bodhidharma walked

out of the court and went to a small monastery in northern China where he spent nine years facing a blank wall. Accounts differ from this point on. Some say that no one paid any attention to him, others that he was besieged by disciples from all over China. But what is agreed upon is the essential theme of his teaching: that the Buddha is not to be found in externals, as in images and acts, but in the heart of man.

Three-quarters of a century have passed. We are in the age of Huinêng (Eno) who taught also that one should look into one's own Buddha nature, since only there could one find prajna, or Supreme Wisdom. A man does not need contemplation, but a return to his own Being.

A monk asked Eno for instruction. "Show me your face before you were born," said Eno.

On another occasion he made an unambiguous statement about his teaching:

My Master had no special instructions for me. He simply insisted on the need for us to see into our own nature with our own efforts. It has nothing to do with meditation or with deliverance. To take hold of the nonduality of Truth is Zen. The Buddha nature we all possess and which we see into is what constitutes Zen. It is indivisible into such opposites as good and evil, eternal and temporal, material and spiritual. To see dualism in life comes from a confusion of thought. The wise, the enlightened see into the reality of things unhampered by erroneous ideas.

Zen has been described as a Chinese reaction to the verbosity and the scholasticism and tediousness of Indian Buddhist thinking. Zen is oblique, unexpected. It twists the mind, confronts the traditional, pushes, baffles, sidesteps, ignores "logical" thought. One cannot *will* his way into enlightenment. It must come unexpectedly, unannounced. Zen puts great emphasis on meditation and avoids images, sacred writings, rites, and an excess of clerical authority. Unlike other Eastern systems, the monks engage in manual labor. Writing, in the form of Scripture or in any other form, is worthless in itself and is valued primarily for what it can lead to. Hüen Sha, for example, was about to preach a sermon when a bird began to sing nearby. He pointed to the bird and remarked that the sermon had just been preached. Another Master, Teu Tse, one day pointed at a stone and said, "In it are all the Buddhas of the past, present and future." Monks should attain enlightenment by their own efforts, by direct experience rather than through that of others.

The king-monk Tran Thai Tong of Vietnam abdicated his throne and went to the mountains in search of a guru. Atop

Mount Yen Tu he found the Venerable
Truc Lam, a Zen Master. Truc Lam said:

*I have lived in the mountain for a long
time and my body has become thin from
a diet of vegetables and fruit, but I can
enjoy walking in the woods and drinking the waters of the springs; I feel as
happy and as free as the clouds. But
what has led your Majesty to give up his
throne?*

*I am aware of the impermanence of
the glory of the throne. I have come
here to seek nothing by the Way to
Buddhahood.*

Truc Lam answered:

*The Buddha is not in the mountain but
in your mind. When your mind is calm
and clear, the Buddha appears. When
your Majesty discovers the true nature
of the mind, then you will attain Buddhahood without going far to seek it.*

I have been writing about Buddhism in
its purest form, as it was and is envi-
sioned not only by the bhikkhu, the
monk, but by the layman. The actual
practice of Buddhism can have serious
defects. The clear vision of Buddha often
has been clouded by hordes of gods and
goddesses, rites and superstitions. The
spread of Buddhism throughout Asia,

peaceful and welcomed as it was, diluted
the original message all too often. Super-

imposed over other religions—Hinduism, nature worship and animism—it
often retained many of their characteristics, absorbing the very same rituals,
spirits, and superstitions that Buddha
himself had condemned and had reacted
against. Instead of replacing nature cults
and local gods, temple rites and a domineering priesthood, Buddhism was forced
to compromise with them. The Sangha,
or brotherhood, which Buddha had conceived as a kind of priestly republic, became in all too many cases a clerical
hierarchy which lived off the layman.
Great monastic complexes arose, in
which the monks had all the privileges
and few of the responsibilities of feudal
landlords. Yet Buddhism flourished and
has retained its original vitality, except
in India where it finally declined in the
face of a Hindu revival; in the twelfth
century A.D. a Muslim onslaught virtually wiped it out. The Buddhists who
remain in India today are from the fringe
areas where India touches on Nepal,
Sikkim, Bhutan and Burma, along with a
few converts from the untouchables.

In other parts of Asia, Buddhism is
having a rivival after having suffered a
decline with a loss of lands and other
secular resources under the rule of the
Western colonial nations. It has become
a Soul-Force in many of the new nations,
and a series of Buddhist Ecumenical
Councils is bringing Buddhists of many
different schools togther for the first
time in history. With modern means of
communication and transportation now
available, Buddhists are now able to

work together in the manner of the West, perhaps without many of the West's problems and difficulties, in a wide move toward purification and renewed growth. The West itself, particularly among intellectuals and young people, has shown a vital interest in Buddhism. While it is unlikely that any Western nation will become Buddhist, there is now the possibility that a substantial number of Westerners may follow the Way, since Buddhism's flexibility allows people to accept its thinking, doctrine, and basic concepts without sacrificing their own culture. With Westerners searching for alternatives to their own personal and national crises, the inexpressible inner reality of Buddhism, sublime and ultimate, has a great appeal.

Orthodox Jews gather at the Wall of the Temple in Jerusalem. This is part of the great temple that King David built, which was later destroyed by the Romans.

JUDAISM

And when Abram was ninety-nine years old, the Lord appeared to Abram and said to him, "I am God Almighty; walk before Me, and be perfect, And I will make My covenant between Me and you and I will multiply you exceedingly." Abram fell on his face and God spoke with him, saying, "As for Me, behold, My covenant is with you, and you shall be the father of a multitude of nations Neither shall your name be called any-more Abram, but your name shall be Abraham, because I have made you the father of a multitude of nations. And I will make you exceedingly fruitful, and I will make nations of you. And I will establish My covenant between Me and you and your seed after you throughout their generations for an everlasting cove-nant, to be God to you and your seed after you. And I will give to you, and to your seed after you, the land of your sojournings, all the land of Canaan, for an everlasting possession, and I will be their God."

Thus, as we read in the Book of Genesis (17:1–8), God speaks to man, to an ancient, gnarled nomad, who by His request, had left his father's house and his kindred when he was seventy-five, and had gone into the land of Canaan. After a long trip, he had settled briefly at a place called Sechem. Here the Lord appeared to Abram and said, "To your descendants I will give this land." The land was occupied by people of other tribes at the time, and it was to be centuries before his "seed" was to be in full possession of it. Abram built an altar at Sechem in honor of the Lord, and another a few miles farther south, near the mountain of Bethel. Then with his flocks and his household (we read in the Bible that among his kinsmen were 318 fighting men) Abram (as he was still called) began to wander south again. On this long trek a number of events took place which were to have untold consequences for Abram and for the world. His wife Sarai (afterward called Sarah) had borne him no children, yet God had promised Abram on several occasions that his descendants would be as multitudinous as the dust of the earth and as many as the stars of the heaven. At the great age of eighty-six, Abram was rewarded by the birth of a son, Ismael, by his wife's slave girl, Hagar. But Ismael was not to be the means of transmission of the special people that were to be God's special favorite (though he is honored among the Muslims as the founder of the Arab peoples). Thirteen years later God promised a doubting Abraham (who had by

Young orthodox Jews study the
Torah, the first five books of the
Bible, in a school in Jerusalem. These
men devote their lives to study, with
the support and encouragement of
their families, and put their religious
studies ahead of secular careers.

now received the special Covenant of the Lord) that he would have a son by his wife Sarah. But Abraham feared that because of his age and Sarah's (she was ninety) no son could be born of them. However, in his hundredth year he became the father of Isaac, through whom God's promise was to be fulfilled.

Abraham wandered on and on. He went into the Negev desert and then (so the Arabs believe) into Arabia to the site of the future city of Mecca, to Egypt and back to the land of Canaan before he settled down. The distances were immense—several thousands of miles—on foot, with herds and kinsmen. Much of the trek was across hostile desert, through hostile peoples who engaged them in skirmishes and battles. The overriding theme of this migratory life was his continuing dialogue with God, testing and sanctifying, rewarding and blessing, demanding his unquestioning loyalty. God made great demands on him, some of which are incomprehensible and can be accepted only as a mystery of the Divine Will, if we try to analyze them objectively. In the greatest test of Abraham's faith, God called upon him to sacrifice his son Isaac as a burnt offering. I find this episode puzzling and disturbing (though it is held up as a supreme example of obedience by Jews, Christians, and Muslims), yet Abraham took Isaac to the top of a mountain (tradition says it was Mount Zion, upon which Jerusalem was later to be founded), built an altar of wood, tied his son and laid him upon the logs. As Abraham raised

Isolation and persecution have been the lot of most Jews since the fall of the Two Kingdoms. The bodies of millions of Jews were burned in ovens (right) after being gassed in German death camps during the Nazi period. The barbed wire fence is symbolic of the barrier that separates Israel from her Arab neighbors.

his knife to sacrifice Isaac, the voice of God called to him, saying not to kill the boy and affirming that He knew that Abraham did not fear Him. Abraham lifted up his eyes and saw a ram caught in a thicket, which he substituted upon the altar for his son.

The Covenant Abraham received from God was not a written document, codified as were the Ten Commandments on tablets of stone and then on parchment rolls, but a promise, an understanding, a statement of God's love, support, friendship. This Covenant, which God also confirms with Abraham's son Isaac and grandson Jacob (Deuteronomy 9:5), binds the Jews to God as a people, as a nation. Through their long years ahead, in their glory, their sufferings, their exiles, their piety and prayer, God is with these Chosen People, mysteriously selected from among the many rather similar nomadic tribes of the primitive Mideast. "I the Lord dwell in your midst," He tells them over and over again, and, "I am the Lord your God; and you shall know that I am the Lord your God." Besides this external transcending friendship, He also has promised them a land —the land of Canaan—in which they may live, to worship Him and to enjoy the grace of being His People. "I will give it to you for a heritage," He says of this land, for "I am the Lord."

The mysterious, everlasting fact is that God has chosen this small tribe from all the wandering tribes of the world to be His People, the Chosen People, a term that for the Jews is an honor beyond all description, and for their enemies a term of jealousy and opprobrium. "For you are a holy people to the Lord your God," says the Book of Deuteronomy (7:16), "the Lord your God has chosen you to be His treasure, out of all the peoples that are upon the earth." The reason given, simply, is that "the Lord has loved you."

The choice of the Jews by God is an enigma, to be explained only in the glory of the heavenly future. The Jews—from the Bible to the present—see no inborn merits in the choice, nothing but the unknowable will of God. The honor is one of unbearable glory, and of grave responsibility. And to be chosen meant also that there had to be a "chooser," that is, God, a Creator who has not dropped from sight after the creation but continues to speak to, to love, to teach the people He has chosen. Thus, as God *is*, the Jews are. The Jews are a reality; the people of Israel, as they came to be known, are a reality of God. Martin Buber, one of the greatest of twentieth-century Jewish theologians, said: "Israel is something existing, something once and for all, unique and unclassifiable by either category or concept. Every pigeon-hole of world history defies attempts at subsuming it." Israel has not succumbed to the forces of the world, to the Egyptians, the Romans, the Christians and the Muslims, to the Spanish Inquisition and Russian pogroms, to Nazi gas chambers, to the secular world. Of this survival, the Jews can call it only a "mystery." "We know that we have not

The Passover Seder. Passover celebrates the liberating flight of the Israelites from Egypt. It is one of the most sacred of all Jewish ceremonies. In Orthodox homes the entire household is purified. Such homes keep separate Passover utensils and dishes which may not be used at other times. At the Seder, the Passover feast, five symbolic foods are displayed: spring greens, a roasted egg, a roasted shank bone of lamb, a bitter herb, and charoset, which is a spread made of finely chopped apples, almonds, raisins, seasoned with a paste of sweet wine. Matzoh, an unleavened bread, which reminds the participants of the haste with which the Israelites left Egypt, is eaten. A goblet of wine is placed at the head of the table for Elijah, the prophet. Prayers and hymns are said, and even folk songs are sung. The Seder is a reliving of the Flight from Egypt and of the entire exile of the Jews from their Promised Land.

been repudiated," wrote Buber. "God's hand holds on to us and does not let us go, holds us into this fire and does not let us fall." Being chosen is "an experiment of God," it is a "unique royal covenant" denied to other peoples. And Who is this God who choses?

God *is*. The Jews do not regard the existence of God as something to be proved. He *is*. He is One, a message repeated again and again. Deuteronomy (6:4) says quite succinctly (in words repeated daily by every Jew who prays), "Hear O Israel, the Lord our God, the Lord is One." But His presence—the Hebrew word is Shekkinah—"fills the universe just as the soul fills the body of man." The world is not God but God is in the world, present for man. When He seems remote it is the fault of sinful man, for God is always ready for those who call upon Him in truth. But this is not to say that God is present in the sense we have seen in Hinduism. What the religion of Abraham teaches about God (as do her daughter religions of Christianity and Islam) is opposite and contradictory to what Hinduism teaches. Where a Hindu sees God everywhere, in himself, in nature, in the heavens, where God surrounds man, envelops and absorbs him and where man is greedy to devour God, to become One with the Divine Essence, Judaism and the other monotheistic religions put God and man at the opposite ends of a divine relationship that clearly distinguishes One from the other. In India God is drawn from the earth, from the skies and the rivers and the seas. He is all and everywhere and with definition and without definition. The Hindu throws himself into God. But in Judaism, God is distinct and different, aloof though loving. He has a single, however incomprehensible, appearance. He is the King of kings and man is His servant. Man stands in fear and trembling, unable to define God. A rabbinical parable puts the problem in these terms:

"An emperor said to Rabbi Joshua ben Hananya: 'I want to see your God.' He replied, 'You cannot see Him.' 'Nevertheless,' the emperor said, 'I want to see Him!' Rabbi Joshua stood the emperor in the summer sun and said, 'Look at the sun.' 'I can't,' said the emperor. Rabbi

Joshua said, 'The sun is but one of the servants who stand in the presence of the Holy One, praised be He, and you cannot look at the sun. Is it not truer that you cannot see the Presence of God?' "

In Hinduism the sun is God in one of His many attributes. And God is also a friend, a neighbor. In His many forms He may play, laugh, bathe, joke, make love. In Judaism, no matter how much we love Him, we must still be in awe of His power and His love. Franz Rosenzweig, a German Jew who wrote early in this century, said, "He wants to be served with trembling and yet rejoices when His children overcome their fear at His wondrous signs." He adds:

Israel intercedes with Him in behalf of the sinning peoples of the world and He afflicts Israel with disease so that those other people may be healed (Isa. 53). Both stand before God: Israel His servant, and the kings of the peoples; and the strands of suffering and guilt, of love and judgment, of sin and atonement, are so inextricably twined that human hands cannot untangle them.

From the time of Abraham onward the dialogue with God developed. His descendants began to settle down with their flocks, in permanent encampments from which they could send out their herds to graze. Always God was with them, loving them, testing, directing, protecting. When a famine sent a number of the Hebrew clans to Egypt (this was about the sixteenth century before the Christian era), they were welcomed and given pasture lands on the eastern side of the Nile delta. Joseph, of the House of Jacob, earned a position of authority under the Hyksos dynasty. Eventually, however, the Hyksos kings were overthrown and expelled, and the Hebrews, or Israelites as they were now also called, along with other foreign minorities, found their favored status at an end. The new rulers turned the Jews into slaves. Some four hundred years later, the tremendous figure of Moses appeared. He is a man of mystery. The Bible tells us that he was a Hebrew who had been found abandoned and was brought up by an Egyptian princess. Moses killed an Egyptian overseer, went into exile, and then, directed by God, returned to help the Israelites escape from Egypt. Again, God was with his people. After a series of terrible trials, the Israelites successfully escaped Egypt, while the Egyptians suffered a number of severe punishments for oppressing the fugitives and for trying to prevent their flight. The Israelites' goal was Canaan, on the southeastern shore of the Mediterranean Sea, the land given to Abraham. Though it was not a particularly attractive or fertile area, it was the Promised Land.

But before gaining the Promised Land, the Israelites were to spend forty years in the wilderness of the triangular Sinai Peninsula, between Egypt and the Red Sea. Today this is a barren and forbid-

In Bombay a diminishing colony of Jews attends the Friday night services. With a shortage of adult males, a woman now performs some of the roles normally done by men. The younger members of the congregation are leaving for Israel, but the older people, too deeply rooted in India, stay on.

ding land; in the past it seems to have had some pleasant fertile valleys, but the vegetation was eaten by wild camels and the woods were cut down by nomads. Even so, at the time of Moses, there was not enough food to support the vast number of Israelite refugees from Egypt. The number, according to the census in the Book of Numbers, is over six hundred thousand men, plus their dependents and servants, some three million in all, which is more than the population of the state of Israel today. To feed this vast number of people God gave them the famous manna.

The route Moses is believed to have taken did not directly lead to Canaan. He went, instead, around the southern perimeter of Sinai, being led, inexorably, to Mount Horeb for his dialogue with God. A medieval writer, Felix Faber (the late fifteenth century), said that before Moses, "No man dared to climb Horeb. It was indeed, even before Moses's time the general belief of mankind that on the summit dwelt the mighty God, whom no one who wished to remain alive could look upon, and whom no one might approach." Faber added: "One of the summits seemed, before Moses's ascent, to glow with powerful fire." Somewhere on these rugged, precipitous cliffs, Moses was given the Law, the Torah, of which the Ten Commandments is the central portion. In turn Moses brought this divine code, which was to be the ruling key to Jewish life, followed with scrupulosity and passion, to the Israelites waiting below.

A bar-mitzvah, the receiving of a Jewish boy into adult Jewish life, takes place at the Wall of the Temple. Women are segregated from men in orthodox Jewish worship; here they peek through the lattice-work at the ceremony.

Moses died in Sinai without ever seeing the Promised Land, but an invasion —for it was a war and not a peaceful migration—brought the Israelites to their new home. There were many battles, some fierce, some mere raids and skirmishes, in which they followed the divine command and seized what God had promised them.

Again we are faced with a mystery. The Bible admits that the land was inhabited by other people, by seven other nations. But these nations had defiled the land by their sins. The ultimate reason, however, is this, as an eleventh-century rabbi, Rashi of Troyes, wrote: "Should the people of the world tell the Jewish people, 'You are robbers, because you took the land of the seven nations of Canaan by force,' they could reply, 'All the world belongs to the Holy One, praised be He. He created it, and gave it to whom He pleased. When He willed, He gave it [the land] to them, and when He willed He took it from them and gave it to us.' " When Mahatma Gandhi expressed the opinion that the Jews of the current era were wrong in trying to resettle the Holy Land at the expense of the Arabs, Martin Buber replied: "It seems to me that God does not give any one portion of the earth away. . . . The conquered land is, in my opinion, only lent even to the conqueror who has settled on it—and God waits to see what he will make of it."

This holy land of Israel—Zion, in the popular term—is given His people by God as a proof of his goodness and love.

The land is flowing with milk and honey; it has abundant water, delicious fruits, minerals, corn and wheat, wine, oil, cattle, goats and sheep, rare spices. It becomes rich, fecund, "God's own treasure," so wealthy that the new inhabitants are able to develop a foreign trade which takes them as far as India. It is a blissful land: "The eyes of the Lord are always upon it." Here each man has a happy home; his "wife is as a fruitful vine" and his "children are like olive plants."

Not all of Canaan was conquered. The struggle went on for centuries; there were Canaanite fortresses and walled cities to contend with, along with pockets of other clans and tribes. The Israelites themselves were especially independent, almost anarchistic, maintaining endless rivalries and feuds with each other. Keeping the social structure unbalanced was the fact that, despite the laws given by God to Moses, the Israelites seemed to be incurably attracted to the pagan cults of their neighbors. Intermarriage with other tribes and participation in their rites began to erode the following of the Law. Even their unity as a people was threatened. Then the magnificent, quarrelsome figure of King Saul pulled the tribes together, giving them both political unity and some sense of their community in the light of God. But Saul and his son Jonathan were cut down in a war with the Philistines, and the crown passed to David. He was anointed king by the men of Judah about the year 955 before the Christian era and seven years later became king over the entire nation of the Israelites.

David was not only a warrior and a poet, the slayer of the giant Goliath and the singer of a number of the Psalms, but a skilled administrator. It was David who established the city of Jerusalem as the capital of the holy land of the Israelites. The city was first called Shalom (or peace) and was the city of the priest-king Melkizadek. (Abraham, rescued from sacrificing Isaac by God, had called the spot yireh or vision.) From the time of David onward it was the most sacred site in the Holy Land, and in exile, it was the yearning for this city that gave the Jews hope. "How shall we sing the Lord's song, in a foreign land," says a Psalm written in Babylonia; "If I forget thee, O Jerusalem," a lament that continued over the centuries.

But the people David had brought together could hardly remain a single nation under his rule. Their natural restlessness, anarchistic tendencies, and mistrust of government began to be asserted. Revolts broke out, and even David's son Absolom rebelled and was put down with difficulty. After a turbulent reign of thirty-three years David died. The succession went to Solomon, one of his younger sons and his own choice for king. Solomon, remembered today for his wisdom and kindness, developed a far-flung overseas trade. The most significant event of his reign was the building of the Temple in Jerusalem to house the sacred Ark of King David. The Temple was part of a sacred com-

The chief rabbi of Jerusalem is surrounded by worshippers as he goes to the Wall to pray for the Jews of Russia.

pound, about 861 feet square, which included not only a holy sanctuary but the royal palace, a combination that was received with misgivings by the prophets of Israel, who feared that the king, incarnating himself in the divine sanctuary, would encroach upon the transcendence of the Lord. The prophet Ezekiel, who described Solomon's Temple in detail, decried the royal desecration of it with "harlotry," "abominations," and the "dead bodies of their kings."

The core of the Temple was an inner sanctuary, a cube some 36 feet in all dimensions, containing the Ark, a sacred object venerated by the northernmost tribes of Israel and carried by David throughout his wars. A door opened to the east, that is, toward the rising sun, onto a courtyard with an altar for burnt offerings where sacrificial rites were performed. Around the Temple were vestibules, hallways, chambers for the priests, stables and storage rooms, and the royal quarters, separated (as Ezekiel lamented) by "only a wall" from the sacred enclosures. The Temple was the national sanctuary, to which all Jews were expected to come on certain festivals "to appear before the Lord." But, as the prophets complained, there were other, lesser shrines throughout the countryside, some of them used for near-pagan purposes.

It was the prophets who maintained the spirit of Israel, who served as the spokesmen for God, clarifying, proclaiming, propagating His word, nagging, bullying, threatening the Israelites into the proper observance of the Covenant they had received from God through Abraham and Moses. This Covenant included not only God's promise to the Chosen People, but the laws He had given them through Moses, the Ten Commandments and a set of other commandments numbering some six hundred and thirteen regulations listed in the book of Leviticus. They include such varied subjects as offerings, the ordination of priests, dietary regulations, the purification of women after childbirth, health measures, defilement from bodily discharges, rituals of holy days, sexual regulations, the calendar, religious vows, and so on.

But there were two types of prophets, the court hangers-on who said what the kings and the people wanted to hear, and the true prophets, who suffered abuse, rejection, and exile. In I Kings 22, for example, we hear of four hundred prophets predicting victory as opposed to one "true" prophet who foretold defeat. The king, Ahab, threw the prophet Micah into prison and then went into battle, disguised, and was slain. When his man washed his war chariot, the dogs licked up his blood and the harlots bathed in it, "according to the word the Lord had spoken" through Micah.

The prophets preached simplicity. In Deuteronomy (30:11 & 14) the Israelites are told: "The commandment which I command this day is not too hard for you, nor is it too far away from you." The message is simple: "The word is very near to you, in your mouth and in

Orthodox students at work in old Jerusalem. The strictest orthodox groups, following the biblical injunction, do not cut their hair or beard, but others follow a more relaxed rule in order to accommodate the modern world.

your heart, that you may do it." The Talmud, the rabbinical commentary on the Torah, says that "After Moses, David came and reduced the six hundred and thirteen commandments to eleven," as in Psalm 15:1–15. But after that Isaiah reduced them to six (Isaiah 33:15), and Micah to three (Micah 6:8), after which Isaiah reduced them to two ("Keep justice and do righteousness"). But Amos made the final reduction: "Thus says the Lord to the house of Israel: Seek Me and live."

But this time the country had split into two warring sections, Israel in the north and Judah in the south. The two states were never happy brothers, though at times they joined against common enemies. In the eighth century before Christ, Israel fell before the Assyrians, who were seeking an outlet to the Mediterranean, and a large number of people were deported. These people, ten of the twelve tribes of the Jews, disappeared from the historical scene. The Assyrians and later the Chaldeans kept hammering away at Judah and it, too, finally fell to the enemy, Jerusalem being captured in 582 B.C. Again, the losers were deported in large numbers to the east, being settled in rich land between the Tigris and Euphrates rivers.

When the Romans destroyed Jerusalem, they marked their victory with the erection of an arch in their capital. The Arch of Titus shows Roman soldiers looting the Temple and carrying off the sacred implements.

Exile in Babylonia was the beginning of the famous Diaspora, or dispersion, of the Jews. There were already Jewish colonies abroad—in the ninth century before Christ a Jewish colony was founded in Damascus and in the following century there began small migrations to Egypt, a land that, despite the horrors of the Exodus, still held an attraction for the Jews. Whenever there was social unrest or the threat of invasion more people fled as refugees to Egypt. The Egyptian city of Alexandria, for example, eventually held a Jewish population of some one million.

The sufferings of the people of Israel were a constant trial which, however, offered an eventual reward. The prophets promised a Messiah, through whom there would come an age of glory and happiness, culminating in an ingathering of all the exiles from the four corners of

Besides the major
groups of Jews from
Europe in Israel, there
are many from smaller
eastern and Asian
nations. Here the
caretaker of the Persian
synagogue shows a
beautiful Torah scroll
his congregation had
brought from Iran.

the earth into the sacred land of Zion. There would be a good material life, a sound political system, and a great age of moral and intellectual development. Man would be perfect in knowledge. This age would include not only the people of Israel but all of mankind united in the One Lord. But this messianic era was not to be easily attained: First there would be times of frightful unrest, with wars, famine, pestilence, and persecution before the final victory of the hosts led by the Messiah.

The Messiah, a "shoot" from the root of the stump of Jesse, the father of King David, is a person of divine gifts; he has supernatural character and ability. The promise of the Messiah rings throughout the prophets, particularly Isaiah, who preaches constantly on this subject. In Isaiah, the Messiah is known as the Wonderful Counselor, Mighty God, Everlasting Father, and Prince of Peace. He will come as a child and the spirit of the Lord will rest upon him. He will bring justice to the poor, and smite the wicked. Opposites will be reconciled— wolf and lamb, leopard and kid goat, calf and lion. Under the Messiah, nations that know not God will run to Him, the Holy One of Israel. In the Prophet Zachariah, the Messiah, the servant of God, is known as the Branch; the people of Israel are told that the Messianic King will, though triumphant and victorious, come humbly riding upon an ass. As the troubles of the Jews increased in the age before the time of Christ and afterward, the longing for the Messiah became more and more poignant. In one disturbance after another, an individual would arise (there are some seventy on record), to announce that he was *the* Messiah, chosen by God as His agent for the deliverance of the Jews. Inevitably the self-proclaimed messiah, after an abortive revolt, would be slain or forced into exile, his followers often maintaining their faith in him in the conviction that he would return later. This messianic longing which, of course, for a few of the people of Israel centered around the figure of Jesus, continued among orthodox Jews into the 1700s.

Less than a century after the restoration of the Temple in Jerusalem by exiles returned from Babylonia, the Persians sent two Jews, Nehemiah and Ezra, to Judah, one as an administrator and the other with a commission over those who practiced Judaism in and around Judah. Both men had been highly influential in the Persian court. What they did now was virtually as forceful and as decisive and as innovative as the actions of Abraham and Moses. As governor of Judah, Nehemiah enacted social reform laws, encouraged and reestablished commerce and industry, and rebuilt the walls of Jerusalem. When Ezra arrived from Babylon, along with 1,800 immigrants, he joined Nehemiah in a reform of their people's religious practices. One of the first steps was a prohibition of intermarriage with outsiders, the first known ban of its kind; the purpose was a purification and a return to the Covenant and the Torah. Ezra had brought with him a revised code of the Torah which was read to the people on regular days (usually market days) and explained in Aramaic, which was now the popular tongue of most of the people. One step, however, was to have a more profound effect upon the future of Judaism (and consequently upon Christianity and Islam when they began) than any other action taken by Nehemiah and Ezra: This was to take religious practices away from the priests and give them directly to the people. In the past, worship had been the role of the priesthood, through sacrifices and prayer in the Temple. But in Babylon there had been no temple, so the people had developed the custom of meeting in the home of a religious leader and reading the sacred books they had brought with them, discussing them and hearing comments on them. During this period of exile, the sacred writings of the past had been collected and edited. A canon of sacred scripture was established. But the Torah was more than a "book." It had a mystic, almost cosmic, conception. When Israel was again to go into exile, the Torah became the center of the nation's secret and avowed desires and aspirations and hopes. The rabbis used to say that "Israel and the Torah are one," and that "The Torah was given only as a means of purifying man." The accepted Jewish view was that the Torah was the "normal way of holiness" for man. In the centuries when in all other cultures literacy

In Jerusalem's Yemenite synagogue a man corrects an old scroll. The ink is prepared from pomegranate seeds.

was the privilege of a very small number of men, it was common for the Jewish male (and women as well) to be able to read. Learning was the most highly praised of all attainments. Even before the destruction of Jerusalem by the Romans, the Jewish elementary school had been established and has survived to the present despite the utmost difficulties.

But the new state of Judah, though controlled by Persia, was not to remain even partially free. It later came under the direct control of the Greeks, the Syrians and then the Romans. The two centuries before the birth of Christ saw almost constant Jewish riots and revolts. The rising of the Maccabees brought a temporary freedom, but the Romans gained control again, ruling with puppet kings. Two major revolts, in A.D. 70 and

אבֿזה עולם ועֿשֿה
מצֿרֿיֿם עֿד בֿא

ומֿשֿה תֿולֿדֿת

הֿלֿדֿם אֿחֿרֿיֿהֿ

בֿלֿולֿם ואֿלֿ טֿ

כֿנֿעֿן בֿדֿרֿך בֿעֿ

ואֿקֿבֿרֿה שֿם בֿ

יֿשֿרֿאֿל אֿת בֿנ

אֿל אֿבֿיו בֿנֿי הֿ

קֿלֿים נֿא אֿלֿי וֿ

לֿא יֿוכֿל לֿדֿאֿ

וֿיֿחֿבֿק לֿהֿם וֿ

פֿלֿלֿתֿי וֿהֿנֿה ה

וֿיֿצֿא יֿסֿף אֿר

אֿרֿצֿה וֿיֿקֿ יֿ

מֿשֿמֿאֿל יֿשֿ

יֿשֿרֿאֿל וֿיֿשֿ

עֿל רֿאֿשֿ אֿפֿ

רֿאֿש מֿנֿשֿה ו

וֿיֿבֿרֿך אֿת יֿ

אֿבֿד לֿפֿנֿי

מֿעֿדֿי עֿד הֿ

יֿבֿרֿך אֿת הֿנֿ

אֿבֿרֿהֿם וֿיֿצ

יֿסֿף כֿי יֿשֿ

וֿירֿע בֿעֿיֿנֿ

רֿאֿש אֿפֿרֿים

אֿבֿיו לֿא כֿן

רֿאֿשֿו וֿיֿמֿא

יֿהֿיֿה לֿעֿם ו

מֿמֿנֿו ורֿעֿ

לֿאֿמֿור בֿך

כֿאֿפֿרֿים וֿכ

וֿיֿאֿמֿר יֿשֿ

אֿלֿהֿים עֿמ

וֿאֿנֿי נֿתֿתֿי ל

מֿיֿד הֿאֿמֿר

וֿיֿקֿרֿא יֿעֿקֿ

אֿת אֿשֿר

וֿשֿמֿעֿו בֿנֿ

רֿאֿובֿן בֿכ

וֿיֿתֿר עֿז פֿ

אֿבֿיך אֿז

שֿמֿעֿון ול

אֿל תֿבֿא

בֿאֿפֿם כֿי א

A.D. 135, against the Romans failed. These ended Jewish hopes for their own state (until 1948 when the British withdrew from Palestine and a provisional national council, meeting at Tel Aviv the same day, May 14, 1948, proclaimed the establishment of the state of Israel. The new state was immediately recognized by the United States and the Soviet Union, and the next day was invaded by the neighboring Arab nations).

The leading scholars who escaped the destruction of the city of Jerusalem in A.D. 70 gathered in a town called Jabne. Under the leadership of a rabbi named Jochanan ben Zakkai they began to assemble and collate all the documents and traditions and commentaries of their predecessors. The immediate fear was that in this terrible disaster Jews around the world (and there was a far larger number of Jews abroad than in Judah) would forget their religion, their heritage, their language and their traditions. A strong system of communal life, based on a very "internal" focus on prayer and study, began to develop. The liturgy, the method of worship, was standardized. No longer did people have to go to the Temple to worship. A group of ten Jewish males was sufficient to form a congregation. Anyone from this congregation could read the Torah to the community. (Normally a male does the reading, but in a declining Jewish community, where there are not enough men, I have heard the Torah read by a woman.) Rules and regulations for each community to follow were established

A hand-lettered Torah from the Yemenite synagogue in Jerusalem. Each synagogue keeps a number of such scrolls and constantly checks them for damage making repairs and corrections as needed.

for its own well-being and for the well-being of all Jews. Each community had its own taxes in addition to those which had to be paid to the secular state. Education was compulsory for males (though women might be educated if they wished), and teachers were to be paid. Active proselytizing ended and soon hope of an immediate recovery of Jerusalem was abandoned, though there was always the distant expectation that someday it would be restored to Judaism—"Tomorrow we will be in Jerusalem." The Temple was now within.

A third-century patriarch named Judah the Prince systematized rabbinical teachings on theological, judicial and practical problems in a code called the Mishnah. Though the Scriptures were basic to Jewish life, the opinion of the rabbis in interpreting the Torah began to assume equal force. Rabbis in Palestine and Babylon started to write Talmuds or Traditions, which were books of commentary on the Torah, to help explain it in the terms of contemporary life and to aid the faithful in applying it to the conditions of a changing world.

Up to the sixth century of the Christian era the Jews lived in "relative" peace, the world being in a chaotic state due to the splitting of the Roman Empire into Eastern and Western empires and the constant attacks of the barbarian tribes upon them. When in 324 the Empire accepted Christianity and established it as the "official" religion, restrictions began to be imposed upon the Jews. Gradually the Church, and thus the state

The two men are praying at the Wall of the Temple.

as its temporal arm, began to become more and more hostile to the Jews. They were seen in various lights: as people to be converted, as the "killers" of Christ, and as a state within the state. From one end of the Christian world to the other, restrictions became increasingly severe. Jews were denied ordinary trades and pursuits like farming and small business. Jews were not allowed to build synagogues or repair old ones. Jews were expelled from one land after another, only to be permitted to return because they were "useful." One of the ten occupations open to them in the Christian world was that of moneylender, a pursuit denied—in theory—to Christians. Since Jews could not own land, their capital was in the form of money or jewels, things to be "borrowed" or expropriated. A strong economic hatred of the Jews was the result, which ran hand-in-hand with the theological anger for the part they were supposed to have played in the Crucifixion. Over and over again theology was used as an excuse for seizing Jewish assets and for persecution. When the knights of Europe set off on the first Crusade in 1095, they "tuned up" by murdering thousands of Jews along the way, on the theory that while the Holy Land might be despoiled by the Muslims, the Jews were equally dangerous. From time to time there were violent anti-Jewish riots. Entire communities would be destroyed or expelled. It is difficult at this date to realize or understand the full horror of life for the Jew in the Christian world, but essentially he

had no rights, no homeland, no means of recourse for wrongs. His salvation came in the intense inner life of the soul, nurtured in the walled communities, the ghettoes (the term is an Italian word) that kept him segregated from the world outside. Within the ghetto, life was intense, prayerful and directed to God, centered on God. God was, in a sense, "one of us," an intimate and close friend and not a distant and avenging judge as He might have been in the distant past. With virtually universal education, ghetto life focused on an intense study of the Torah and the Talmud. The emphasis was on prayer, either communal (three times a day) or individual. The priesthood had disappeared. Judaism was now a lay religion practiced by individuals in a solidly established community.

But the liberating movements of the eighteenth and nineteenth centuries gave a new turn to Judaism. Once America opened her shores to the world, Jews began to migrate in large numbers. Tens of thousands walked from Russia and Russian-occupied Poland and Lithuania across Europe to take a ship from one of the western seaports. German Jews also came by the tens of thousands, and Jews from all the other ghettoes of Europe. Though all shared a common religion and a common background, Jews from Eastern Europe and those from Western Europe found that they had different traditions, which brought new tensions in America. Eastern European Jews were strongly orthodox, following the Torah

The side curls and black hats indicate young jews of strict orthodoxy.

to the letter. Western European Jews had often been in a halfway position in Germany and France; they had reformed and liberalized their worship and were becoming secularized.

In America the tremendous pent-up energies that had been repressed by the ghetto began to be unleashed as Jews entered into the mainstream of American life. Today the practice of Judaism as a religion has undergone wide changes, becoming (though perhaps only in externals) less rigorous, somewhat secular, much more relaxed. The majority of Jews in the West do not observe the Torah in the literal sense (for example, in not following the dietary laws, and other observances such as not cutting the beard and hair). Many practice Judaism only on certain holy days, such as Yom Kippur, the Day of Atonement. Daily worship (that is, the morning, noon and evening prayer) is rare, and even the popular Friday night attendance at the synagogue is observed virtually only by the most orthodox. But despite these changes, Judaism still retains its creative spirit and energy, the loving touch of the people whom God chose mysteriously from among the nomadic tribes of the Middle East.

THE ESSENCE OF JUDAISM. To lead a "Torah-true" life—that is the essence of Judaism. To pray three times a day. To follow that most ancient Jewish ritual, circumcision. "The Israelites who came out of Egypt faithfully observed one commandment: they circumcised their infant sons," says an old commentary. "The Egyptians told them: Why must you circumcise your sons? Let them grow up like Egyptians and you will eventually take the heavy load of slavery off your shoulders. The Israelites answered: Did Abraham, Isaac and Jacob forget their Father in heaven? Should their children forget Him?" Abraham was not called "perfect" until he was circumcised.

And marriage. "The whole world depends on the holiness of the union between man and woman, for the world was created for the sake of God's glory and the essential revelation of His glory through the increase of mankind," said Rabbi Nahman of Bratislava. "In truth all experiences of the Divine Unity and Holiness depend on the union between man and woman, for the ultimate meaning of this act is very lofty. . . . Through the act of union in holiness . . . and purity life is increased and years are added. Through it 'man sees life with his wife' and attains wisdom and elevation of the spirit." The rabbi stresses, it will be noticed, union "in holiness and purity." In marriage, says another rabbi, "No man may abstain from fulfilling the commandment 'Be fruitful and multiply.' " The rabbis are divided about the number of children needed to fulfill the commandment. Some say that "children" means two sons, others, a son and a daughter. Judaism alone among the major religions discourages—forbids—the celibate life, the childless marriage.

 The most pervasive of Jewish laws are those concerning kasruth, or dietary regulations, pertaining to permitted and forbidden foods. "Ultimately," says a contemporary rabbi, "they cannot be rationalized. The believer accepts them as part of a total system, the Jewish way to holiness, ordained by God." The laws are extensive: You shall not boil a kid in its mother's milk. You may eat cloven-footed, cud-chewing animals (such as the cow), but not hooved, cud-chewing animals (such as the camel). Among water creatures you may eat whatever has fins and scales, but not what has no fins or scales. Flesh may not be served on the table together with milk products. Animals that die of themselves may not be eaten, nor animals that have certain injuries or wounds. The great Spanish Jewish theologian Moses Maimonides said:

The Law enjoins that the death of the animal should be the easiest. It is not allowed to torment the animal by cutting the throat in a clumsy manner, by pole-axing, or by cutting off a limb while the animal is still alive. It is also prohibited to kill an animal and its young on the same day (Leviticus 22:28), in order that people should be restrained and prevented from killing the two together in such a manner that the young is slain in the sight of the other, for the pain of the animals in such circumstances is very great.

And charity. The obligation to help one's fellowman has been binding since the Law was received by Moses. To let your land lie fallow every seven years so that not only the poor may eat from it but also the wild beasts. To forgive debts, to pay tithes, to open your hand to the stranger, to feed the widow, to ransom captives (a great necessity in the Christian Middle Ages). Whatever the cause, generosity to the poor and the unfortunate by Jews has never been surpassed.

His throne radiates before Him and His palace is full of splendor.

With a gleam of His ray He encompasses the sky, His splendor radiates from the heights.

Abysses flame from His mouth, and firmaments sparkle from His body.

Orthodoxy is strict about cleanliness. The cup has two handles, because to touch a handle held by an unwashed hand would pollute the washed hand again.

Such is the image of the Divine Palace and the Throne of God as seen by one of the mystics of the second exile. In the days of the prophets the gap between God and man was clear—God spoke through the prophets; they were His messengers to the world, solitary individuals serving to transmit His word. "The Lord put forth His hand to touch my mouth," said Jeremiah. With the mystic the situation is different; his aim is to ascend to Heaven during his own lifetime. He seeks union with God as an end in itself. Whether or not the world exists is often of little interest to him. This is not to deny a certain mystical strain throughout the Hebrew prophets —Isaiah and Ezekiel, for example, speak of visions of God which came to them during states of ecstasy. After a particular vision Ezekiel remained a week in a state of "utter stupefaction, dumb and motionless."

The mystic seeks not to serve as a channel of communication but to ascend to the Divine Palace in the vision of and the love of God. Jewish mysticism was slow to develop, not beginning in the classical sense until after the fall of Jerusalem, when a movement known as Merkabah, or Chariot mysticism, arose, inspired by the prophetical vision of Ezekiel. In images of fire and light, the mystic seeks to ascend to the Divine Throne to seek the Face of God which is ablaze with the splendor of unbearable light.

This image of fire, of consuming, all-pervading light was constant during the first centuries of the Merkabah movement. Rabbi Eliezer ben Arach was expounding the mysteries of the Chariot to Rabbi Jochanan ben Zakkai (who is said to have been the founder of the movement) when the fire came down from heaven and danced among the trees of the fields. From the flames an angel spoke to the rabbis. In another example, while Rabbi Jonathan ben Uziel was studying the Torah, every bird that flew overhead was burned by fire. The mystics rode the fiery chariot to heaven even while alive, as Enoch and Abraham had done before them. A body of sacred writings developed on the theme of rabbis who entered heaven, and of men who hoped for the experience, which was prepared for by prayer, study, fasting, and other ascetic practices, and even

DEAR VISITOR, YOU ARE QUITE WELCOME TO MEAH SHEARIM, BUT PLEASE DO
NOT ANTAGONIZE OUR RELIGIOUS INHABITANTS BY STROLLING THROUGH
OUR STREETS IN IMMODEST CLOTHING. OUR TORAH REQUIRES THE JEWISH
WOMAN TO BE ATTIRED IN MODEST DRESS. MODEST DRESS; DRESS
SLEEVES REACHING UNTIL BELOW THE ELBOWS, (SLACKS FORBIDDEN)
STOCKINGS, MARRIED WOMEN HAVING THEIR HAIR COVERED, ETC., ARE
THE VIRTUES OF THE JEWISH WOMAN THROUGHOUT THE AGES. PLEASE DO NOT
OFFEND OUR RESIDENTS AND CAUSE YOURSELF ANY UNNECESSARY INCONVENIENCE.
WE BEG YOU NOT TO INFRINGE UPON OUR WAY OF LIFE AND "HOLY CODE OF LAW".
WE BESEECH YOU TO USE DISCRETION BY NOT TRESPASSING OUR STREETS IN AN
UNDESIRED FASHION. THE MEN ARE REQUESTED NOT TO ENTER BAREHEADED.
THANKING YOU IN ADVANCE FOR COMPLYING WITH OUR REQUEST AND WISHING YOU BLESSINGS FROM ABOVE FOR YOUR GOOD DEED,
COMMITTEE FOR GUARDING MODESTY, MEAH SHEARIM AND VICINITY, JERUSALEM, THE HOLY CITY A'S DIR

GIVE THE JEWS IN ISRAEL
RELIGIOUS LIBERTY
DOCTORS CUT UP JEWISH BONES
AND STEAL THEIR ORGANS
CONTRARY TO JEWISH LAW
ISRAELI LAW and ORDINARY DECENCY
PUT THEM ON TRIAL !

The entrance to the Orthodox quarter of Jerusalem reminds
the more reformed Israeli that he is entering an area sacred to
strict Jews. The quarter is locked at night, and observes the
Sabbath laws and regulations to the letter.

by the use of magic names, numbers and drawings and seals. One book, for example, The Book of Creation, taught a mysticism of the letters of the Hebrew alphabet on the assumption that since Hebrew is a sacred language, the sacred language, it is also the language of creation.

In the Middle Ages the Hasidic sects began to emerge. The word hasid means pious, devout or godly, and where the Merkabah mystics taught a visionary and ecstatic life, the Hasidim put their emphasis on a life of devotion and learning which found its fulfillment in the Divine Immanence. "God fills the ether," said a German Hasid of the thirteenth century. "Everything is in Him, and He sees everything." Another said that God is the Soul of the soul. A profound otherworldliness and asceticism developed. A mysticism of suffering and penance was taught. "Those who are truly just," said a Hasid, "take sufferings upon themselves for their generations." It was believed that the presence of only twelve just men would save the world from God's wrath for its sins. The forgetfulness of the self, union with God through the practice of prayer, were the themes that ran through medieval Hasidism.

A new kind of Hasidism arose in the seventeenth century with the saintly Ukrainian rabbi, Israel ben Eliezer, who was more popularly known as Baal Shem Tov, the Master of the Good Name. His was a time of great social unrest and severe repression of the Jews. Baal Shem Tov never wrote a word in his life, but

Young orthodox students take a break between classes. Their lives are devoted to an almost uninterrupted study of the Torah and Talmud.

his followers recorded his sayings and his miracles. His parents died before he was six and the community put him into school, as the Talmud required. His early life was spent in the wilderness in terrible poverty, performing miracles (we read of him healing the sick, walking on water, causing a tree to burn by a mere glance, saving a prostitute from being stoned). He had a divine radiance which encompassed him wherever he went. His disciples said he spoke directly to God and could intervene for lost souls. When he died in 1760 he had an estimated 100,000 followers, half the Jews of Europe. But he was also despised and hated, and Baal Shem Tov and the Hasidic movement, which still exists today, are often looked upon as outdated and irrelevant. (One modern historian calls Hasidism "A triumph of ignorance over knowledge.") After his death the Hasidic movement split into sections and weakened, but found itself in an awakening in this century, particularly after World War II, when many of the few surviving Jews of East Europe were able to come to America. There are now several Hasidic groups in Brooklyn, New York, the most vital of which are the Lubavitchers, who claim to be the inheritors of the original Baal Shem Tov, tracing their descent through seven rebbes (leaders).

The Lubavitcher ideal is the traditional Torah-true life, that is, to follow the 613 laws and prescriptions of the Torah even in the midst of the modern world. The Lubavitchers believe that in every man there is a spark that burns as long as he lives, no matter how isolated he is from other Jews or how far away he is from religious practices. To awaken this spark young teams of Lubavitchers go out periodically to visit Jewish families and communities who may be isolated from other Jews. Though Lubavitchers live in their own communities, they do not try to reestablish ghettoes. What they try to do is to establish a "hallowed" atmosphere within themselves in order to nurture the divine spark.

Hasidism developed a number of mystical leaders, the zaddiks, who were more like gurus or yogis than rabbis. They gained tremendous personal power which was sometimes abused by taking advantage of less sophisticated followers. The Hasidim were in endless conflicts with the synagogue and established Judaism. When the Hasidim got the upper hand in a community they often ousted the rabbi. When they were in a minority they were persecuted and their synagogues closed. The violent opposition from the orthodox was led by a rather remarkable man, Elijah of Vilna, whose followers gave him the ancient Babylonian title of Gaon. The Gaon said that the true joy of worship was not in ignoring the printed word and in trying to be a mystic but in the profound study of the sacred Word. The Gaon himself was a genius, having mastered the Torah by the age of eight and the Talmud by nine. At ten he turned to science but his father put him back to the Talmud. Though he himself was not a rabbi, the Gaon excommunicated the Hasidim, calling them "Jewish illiterates." He stressed the need of learning, particularly of science, and put his students to translating scientific books into Hebrew.

It wasn't until the nineteenth century that the eternal longing for Zion took a physical form. A few Jews had always survived in the Holy Land, buffeted by Romans, the Crusaders, and the Muslims. In the nineteenth century, Palestine, as the land was now being called, became the goal of a trickle of Jewish immigrants, many of them intellectuals, who saw no solution to the Diaspora but a full return to Zion. The movement coalesced around a Central European Jew named Theodor Herzl, who held the first Zionist Congress in Switzerland in 1897. His plan was to buy large tracts of land in Palestine and settle Jews upon them, a scheme that drew much of its support from the very poor, the very orthodox and the intellectuals but was opposed by many assimilationist and reform Jews. The return to Zion became a physical, mystical goal. By 1948 (Palestine was now under British rule), the Zionists had bought a quarter of a million acres of land and settled 83,000 immigrants in over two hundred newly founded villages, reclaiming the land from barren desert; the project included the planting of five million trees. Meanwhile other immigrants—some legal, many illegal, many refugees from Nazi Germany—flooded into Palestine, so that in 1948 the population numbered over three-

quarters of a million people, this in addition to some six hundred thousand Arabs in the area. The Zionists wanted an independent state, the Arabs resented the Zionist intrusion; there was violence and bloodshed between Jews, Arabs and the British—a situation too complicated and fraught with emotion to detail here. In an explosion that shook the Middle East, the Jews proclaimed the state of Israel on May 14, 1948, and as the British departed, tens of thousands of Palestinian Arabs fled, and the surrounding Arab nations sent their armies into the new nation. The crisis is not yet solved. For many Jews Israel connotes the return to Zion but for the very strictly orthodox it is just another secular nation and Zion is still to come. Meanwhile the stand-off between Israel and the Muslims drains everyone's energies.

Today, world Judaism is at a beginning of a new era in its glorious and tragic life. The searing persecution under the Russians in the nineteenth century, which eroded Eastern European Judaism, and the Final Solution of the Nazis in World War II, in which some six million Jews were murdered, generally put an end to the Hasidic way of life; orthodoxy itself has declined. With the creation of the state of Israel and the "emancipation" of Jews in the Western world, Judaism and the Jews face challenges as great as any in the past. Contradictory currents are running strong and deep: secularism and assimilation, the New Zion of Israel, the struggle to maintain a Torah-true life in an increasingly unorthodox world.

Atop Mount Zion, sacred to King David, young and old celebrate the Feast of Lights, Hanukkah.

ISLAM

✿ *LĀ-ILĀHĀ-ILLĀ-ĀLLĀH*
There is no god but God.

Five times a day the Muslim turns toward Mecca, the holy city where the Prophet Muhammad first received the Message from God that He alone was supreme, to testify to the great truth of that Message. LĀ-ILĀHĀ-ILLĀ-ĀLLĀH. "There is no god but God," cries the muezzin from the top of the minaret as he calls the faithful to worship. LĀ-ILĀHĀ-ILLĀ-ĀLLĀH, says each man as he prays in the ritual that is commanded five times a day, day in and day out, for a man's entire life. At dawn, when the sky is beginning to clear but before the sun has risen, at noon when the sun is starkly overhead, in the late hours of the afternoon, immediately before the sun sets, and at night before going to sleep (but not later than midnight) the Muslim prays. I have seen a Muslim put down his prayer rug on a traffic island in a main street in Tehran, ignoring the cars that roared past him, also in a garage on the Gaza Strip, in the desert in southern

Jordan, in a downtown mosque in the highly sophisticated city of Beirut, and in a converted New York town house. This prayer, this witness to God, this beseeching of the Almighty of submission to the Divine is the central fact of Islam. Nothing else matters. Everything— love, charity, knowledge, mysticism, the law, the family and the state—flows from this one act of submission, Islam. Islam itself means "submission," and Muslims are "those who submit."

Everything has been stripped away. One needs only the barest essentials; in fact, one needs nothing, not even a prayer rug, to worship, to make that direct communicaton to God that is Islam. Islam is man alone with God. All else is irrelevant.

It is Ramadan, already traditional among the Arabs of the great barren peninsula as a month of fasting. The Angel Jibril comes to Muhammad and says:

"Recite!"

Muhammad asks: "What Shall I recite?"

The order is repeated three times, until the Angel says:

"Recite in the name of your Lord, the Creator, Who created man from clots of blood.

"Recite! Your Lord is the most bountiful One Who by the pen has taught mankind things they did not know."

When Muhammad awoke (for this happened in a dream), these words seemed to be inscribed upon his heart.

Left. In downtown
Beirut, Lebanon, amid
the roar of traffic,
a man in a mosque
bows down in prayer.

Above. In central Iran
three students for the
priesthood meet in a
mosque to discuss the
Qur'an.

Right. Face on the
ground, a man debases
himself before God. This
submission to the Divine
is the meaning of Islam.

In its expansion through the Mediterranean and the Middle
East Islam took over and converted many Christian churches.
This is a former Catholic basilica in Constantinople, now
Istanbul, converted into a mosque.

With this incident we have the beginning of the Qur'an (or Koran), the great book of revelation of Islam and the beginning of Muhammad's reception of the Divine Message. The Arabic word Qur'an means "the recital." For Muslims it is the infallible word of God, revealed to the Prophet Muhammad by the Angel Jibril (or Gabriel). Except for the opening surah (or chapter) and a few later passages in which either the Angel or the Prophet speaks in the first person, it is God Himself who speaks throughout.

The first appearance of Jibril came about the year 610 of the Christian era, when Muhammad was about forty. Muhammad was born in about 570 (the exact dates of his early life are imprecise) in Mecca, a trading city in Arabia. His father had died before he was born, as did his mother soon afterward. His family had been poor though respectable. He was raised by his uncle, who defended his nephew against critics but could never accept his ideas. Muhammad's early years are unknown, though there is a tradition that he went to Syria with a trading caravan when he was in his teens—in other words, he had "foreign" experience. He was known as an exceptionally honest and moral person, and his reputation led a widow named Khadijah to put him in charge of her family business (they were traders). At the age of twenty-five Muhammad married her, though she was fifteen years older. (After her death he married again, at the age of fifty.)

Muhammad's marriage to Khadijah was a happy one, and he became successful in business and earned a reputation for growing wisdom and virtue. Eventually he became a contemplative, periodically retiring to a cave outside Mecca where he spent long hours in meditation and prayer. At the age of forty he experienced his first revelation. Jibril's initial visit confused and amazed him, but eventually he grew to accept the fact that the Angel was none other than the messenger of God, Allah, the Creator and Sustainer of the world, the One Who has no partner. Over the years the main principles of the new religion, henceforth known as Islam, were revealed to Muhammad. He was told he was the last of the prophets and that he was charged with the responsibility of bringing this final revelation of the Lord to the world. Islam became the last of the great world religions to appear, and with it a new era in the history of mankind began.

There are secular explanations for Muhammad's mission to the world, but in the end, one must attribute it to a divine call, which cut through the various rather confused religious beliefs of the Meccans and the neighboring tribes. The situation was further confused by the proselytizing of both Jews and Christians, who did not get along with each other, and also saw the Arabs as pagans. The old belief of the Oneness of God was strong, but at times the people's adherence to tribal and animistic gods ran with greater force. Muhammad's insistence on "One God and no other God but God" presented a challenge that was hard to accept. Not only did he offend his own people, but the Jews and Christians as well, who saw this kind of monotheism as an affront to their own interpretation. But in the long run, it was Muhammad's insight which was to win out, in Arabia and then the Middle East and other large parts of the world.

Mecca was a small trading town, ruled by a wealthy and well-entrenched commercial aristocracy. It lay in a barren rocky valley forty-eight miles east of the Red Sea, midway between Syria in the north and Yemen in the south. Across the sea was Abyssinia, one of the first countries to be converted to Christianity. Mecca lay on the trade route from southern Arabia to Damascus in the north and to Baghdad in the east. Each winter a large caravan passed through Mecca on its way south; in the summer it returned to Damascus. Dates, incense, jewels from India and silks from China passed through Mecca. The city was urbane, sophisticated, rich. During the year there were four sacred months in which fighting, raiding and bloodshed were forbidden.

Mecca was old when Muhammad was born. A tradition among the Arabs of the peninsula is that it was Adam who first stood there. Adam is said to have constructed the Ka'ba, the structure which is the central shrine of Mecca and of all Islam, based upon a house of worship in Paradise, where angels endlessly praised the Lord God while circumambulating the shrine. Inside the Ka'ba is the Black Stone, embedded in a silver setting. The Stone is not actually black, according to pilgrim accounts I have read, but of a dark amber color, and moreover "not stone nor metallic," but of "an entirely unfamiliar substance" with "perceptible characteristics which defy definition." In his wanderings the prophet Ibrahim (or Abraham) visited the Ka'ba and left his slave girl Hajar (or Hagar) there along with his son Ismail (or Ismael). Ibrahim rebuilt the Ka'ba, and it became a center of pilgrimage for the Arabs of the peninsula, even at the time when they were worshipping various gods, and eventually for all Muslims. The creed that Ibrahim and Ismail left behind was followed by the people around Mecca for centuries, but gradually the concept of Allah as the Supreme Being was diluted by the practice of worshipping various other gods, manifested in idols of stone or wood. Some three hundred idols were clustered around the Ka'ba; the main deities represented the sun, moon and planets; the lesser ones were tribal totems.

It is the urban character of Mecca which has led some critics to say that Islam is not a true religion of the desert. But Mecca lies adjacent to barren, ancient mountains, forbidding and stark. It was small in Muhammad's time, and even now cities in the Middle East are often hardly more than enlarged oases in the midst of forbidding land: bare rocks, sand, long plains of scraggly vegetation. And hovering above all is the

Islam is a religion of the desert, though many Muslims live in urban areas. But the great arc from west Africa, to the Middle East, to Pakistan and the Asia steppes, is largely arid land, relieved by fertile oases and villages, towns and cities.

burning sun that parches and dries and brings hallucinations of running streams and limpid pools to the traveler and the city dweller alike. Usually a Middle Eastern city begins and stops abruptly; there are no suburbs, in the Western sense, no green belts. One has merely to stroll past the last mud or stone house into burn-

ing sand and sheets of eroded rock. The same wind storms and sand storms, the same piercing sun strike "city" and desert alike. There is, however, a psychological difference between the physical closeness of tightly packed houses, narrow streets, and teeming markets, and the vast, endless spaces beyond that are nothing more than a hard-surfaced ocean. Islam has had its greatest appeal in barren, open lands, in sun-struck, parched corners of the earth—Arabia, North Africa, the Middle East, Turkey, and Persia, the burning emptiness of India and what is now Pakistan. When it found its way into the hearts of the nomads of the Asian steppes, it lodged among people who used the trackless spaces as other men might the ocean. It is the greatest dimension of space, of the purity and starkness of emptiness, of man alone in nothing, that underscores the tremendous gap between man and God that is the running theme of Islam.

IN THE NAME OF GOD
~THE COMPASSIONATE
~THE MERCIFUL

Praise be to God, Lord of the Creation,
the Compassionate, the Merciful,
King of the Last Judgment!
You alone we worship, to You alone
we pray for help.
Guide us to the straight path,
the path of those whom You have favored
not of those who have brought your wrath
nor of those who have gone astray.

As the revelations progressed, what was Muhammad to do? He saw that he was being given a new, a clear vision of God and he felt that he was being asked to preach to his fellow men. Jibril told him he was being given a "burdensome call." He began to preach to the Meccans, endlessly, as the revelations came to him, but he met with fierce opposition. His hearers feared his challenge, not only to their traditional beliefs but even to the structure of their society, which was commercial and exploitive of others. Muhammad asked for social justice as well as for an end to usury and to whatever set one man against another and harmed the poor. He was accused of being a magician, of being possessed by demons. When he was being rejected and laughed at by the Meccans, his wife, Khadijah, supported him. "When I was poor she enriched me," he said. "When all the world abandoned me she comforted me, and when I was called a liar she believed in me."

During the first three years the only progress he achieved was in the conversion of his closest friends and a few Meccans. But when he broadened his preaching after Jibril told him to "proclaim what you have been commanded, without fear of the heathen," the city still rejected him. He was laughed at when he preached the resurrection of the body and told the people about heaven and hell. He taught that in the end man was to be judged by his acts, and that he was answerable to God for them. The unrighteous (for man is re-

bellious, a hardened and confirmed rebel) faced impending doom. And above all, said Muhammad, man must pray, he must pray constantly, unceasingly. Some of the Meccans suggested that he soften his teaching, that he compromise. He refused. He was being given a divine revelation, which was not being accepted. It was his duty not to surrender to frustration but to succeed. But after thirteen years, he had only a small band of followers. He seemed to have reached a deadlock.

However, Muhammad's message of integrity, of idealism, sanctity and love had not languished in isolation. Mecca's neighboring city of Medina had heard of his doctrines and had been receptive to them. The city was in the midst of a great turmoil and he was asked to mediate. At the same time, his enemies among the Meccans were conspiring to murder him, so it seemed wise for Muhammad to leave Mecca. He took a small band of followers and fled to Medina. This flight is known as the Hejira, or migration, and marks the beginning of the Muslim calendar. (The Christian date was A.D. 622.)

In Medina the revelations continued, becoming deeper and being accompanied by inner struggles which were sometimes manifested by physical symptoms resembling epilepsy. There was no pattern to the revelations; they came at various times. When Muhammad felt that the mystical contact was approaching, he shivered and trembled and covered himself with a heavy shawl. Un-

Even in the midst of the desert, the Muslim made the most of water and greenery, developing new forms of architecture which enabled him to worship God in the utmost simplicity.

der it he could be heard groaning and puffing and uttering hoarse cries. These actions have brought the criticism that he was an epileptic, as if to say that a sick man—which he was not—could not bear a true witness to the Divine. But Muhammad had shown no signs of epilepsy before the revelations, and no signs of it otherwise; the physical stresses came only when he was experiencing revelations and not without them. I mention this point because his critics have tried to dismiss Muhammad and his message on this physical basis.

Sometimes he heard vague voices or rustling sounds; on other occasions Jibril appeared directly to him. Muhammad told his disciples what he had heard and experienced, and the revelations were memorized. Many surahs, or chapters, of the Qur'an were received in fragments. Eventually they were written down on whatever was available, such as animal skins, palm leaves, bits of pottery and even the shoulder blades of sheep (paper had not yet been brought westward from China). After Muhammad's death, these revelations were gathered in surahs, and when the final reconciliation was made, they were arranged in order of length, in most cases the longest coming first, and the shortest, last. This arrangement has caused a great amount of difficulty to scholars and theologians in attempting to unravel the progression of the revelations to Muhammad. Within twenty years of Muhammad's death, at a time when several of his followers still knew the entire revelation by heart, an "official" vulgate edition was made from copies in the care of Muhammad's widow, and all others were destroyed by fire. Copies were made of this edition and distributed to the five major cities under Muslim rule: Medina, Mecca, Basrah, Kufah and Damascus.

Medina had a large Jewish colony; Muhammad drew up a charter guaranteeing the Jews religious freedom, and asked Jews and Muslims to work for peace and order. But whatever peace and order was gained through Muhammad's mediation was only temporary. Though he was well received in Medina, his primary thought was still the conversion of the Meccans. After Muhammad and his followers left Mecca, the Meccans seized their property and began to harass Muslims from Medina along the trade routes. During the next few years there was a series of wars with the Meccans, with the Jews, who were expelled, and with Bedouin tribesmen. Six years after the Hejira, Muhammad decided to approach Mecca peacefully, since the majority of the city's people now seemed to favor Islam. This return, a kind of pilgrimage, is known as the rite of 'umra. However, it took two years of negotiations with the city leaders, while Muhammad and his people camped outside Mecca, before he was received peacefully. Almost all of Mecca accepted Islam, and the entire Arabian peninsula now lay open to Muhammad. "With

The Great Mosque of Damascus. The shrine (center) is said to contain the head of Saint John the Baptist. The group of men (left) is studying the Qur'an.

God's help victory came," says the Qur'an of this great event, the conversion of the Meccans, "and you see men embrace His faith in multitudes, give glory to your Lord and seek His pardon. He is ever disposed to mercy."

Now most of Arabia submitted to Islam, some of the tribes, though, being converted by military force. Though Mecca was the "holy" city, Muhammad made Medina the seat of his operations. Then suddenly, while preparing for a compaign against the Christian Arabs of Transjordan, Muhammad was taken by a fever and died. It was the eleventh year after the Hejira, or A.D. 632. Within a century, the Qur'an was being read across half the known world, from the valleys of southern France to India and the vast steppes of Asia, stopping short of the Great Wall of China. Islam shot outward like a series of comets, touching the human soul in a way that not even Buddhism or Christianity had achieved earlier. There seemed to be no barriers to Islam: Christians, Hindus, Zoroastrians, Buddhists, animists, all left their ancestral religions to submit to God as the Muslims preached Him. The facile explanation that the Muslim conquest came as the result of a fanatical application of the sword does not hold true, though it may be valid in some situations. Islam kept the allegiance of the people it converted, despite long periods of dissolution, irresolution, weakness, decadence and social upheaval. Though the Muslim countries might be far apart politically, they have a common spiritual and even cultural bond that unites them into an Islamic brotherhood which is stronger than any other world religion.

God is the light of the heavens and the earth. His light is like a niche that enshrines a lamp, the lamp itself being within a crystal with the brilliance of a star, lit from a blessed olive tree that is neither eastern nor western, whose oil gives light almost as though no fire has touched it. Light upon light. God guides to His light whomever He wills.

Muhammad's death left his followers in a political crisis. Religion, at least for the present, was not an issue—it had been declared through the Qur'an that the religion of Islam had been completely revealed and that Muhammad's purpose had been fully accomplished. But the Islamic community, engaged in a series of wars, needed a leader. There were not only military but political, civil, economic and social problems to be solved. Muhammad's Companions (as they are known) assembled and solemnly discussed the need for a khalif, or successor of the Prophet, from among their own group. The man selected was Abu Bakr, a merchant, the oldest of the Companions, and famed as the first adult male ever to accept Islam. He was given the title of Khalifat Rasul Allah, the Successor of the Messenger of God. One of his first moves was to put down a series of tribal revolts in Arabia. Theologically,

A pool for washing is a requirement for every mosque. Here, face, hands and feet must be washed before worship. Water must be running, and if water is not available, as in the desert, sand may be used.

perhaps his most important act was to collect all the written documents, the verses of the Qur'an and the other written records, from Muhammad's time. The attempt to form a stable leadership failed: the next three khalifs were assassinated during the endless civil disturbances that shook Arabia. The fourth khalif, Ali ben Abu Talib, who was both cousin and son-in-law of Muhammad (he had married the Prophet's daughter Fatima), transferred the seat of government from Medina to Iraq. Ali was the last of the so-called Righteous Khalifs, the original Companions, and after his death a new line began. Soon the style of Islam became heavily political, subordinating religion to secular needs. A Meccan family, the Umayyads, assumed the khalifate, ruling for less than ninety years. They were replaced by a non-Arab family, the Abbasids, who (to reduce Islamic history of that time to a simple catch-all phrase) gave Islam its Arabian-nights flavor during a reign that lasted until the middle of the thirteenth century. There was not only intrigue, murder, civil strife and war, but also at the same time great theological development. Islamic culture flowered with the growth of mystical movements and imaginative scholarship. The brief Umayyad dynasty had given Islam unity, but the Abbasids produced a highly complex society. In the end, as the result of the endless intrigues and the relentless shifting of political sands, the khalifs became little more than figureheads controlled by powerful, unscrupulous wazirs, or

Islam is making great numbers of converts in Africa, either among Animists and other people considered pagan, or among tribes that were Christianized earlier.

prime ministers. The influence of the Arabs faded away, and Byzantine Greeks, Persians, and Turks came to control the court. With the decline of the Abbasids, the Islamic world split into dozens of khalifates, emirates and sultanates. Meanwhile the religious life, which is what concerns us most, developed with the same vitality that Islam had shown during the feverish expansion of its first century.

THE TEACHINGS OF ISLAM. God—God alone—is the central theme of Islam. All else is irrelevant. The existence and survival of all living creatures, of the world itself, is due to God, Who is the only God and Who is deserving of all our worship. God created man and all that is in the world for the service of man (Judaism and Christianity teach the same). Man cannot set other gods in partnership with God. Superstitions and magic (though such practices exist in Islam as in other religions) are contrary to God and His omnipotence. The orderly processes of nature and the world are signs of the existence of God. "God is eternal, has no beginning and no end," says a Muslim commentator in a phrase that resounds not only through all of Islamic belief but Jewish and Christian as well. "He is self-subsistent and is One in all respects: nothing resembles Him. Everyone and everything depend on Him, but He depends on none and is not in need of anything. He is all life; He is seeing; He is hearing; He is speaking; He is omnipotent; He is omniscient;

He causes things to be according to His benevolent will." Thus we know God and reach Him through His creation.

God is omnipotent but man is fallible, weak, quavering, sinful. Man easily goes astray. To guide His people on the right path, to save man from damnation, God has selected certain righteous individuals, the prophets (or nabis in Arabic) through whom He speaks in direct revelation. There have been a number of nabis—witnessed by the Torah, the Old and New Testaments—beginning with Adam and proceeding through Noah, Abraham, Ishmael, Isaac, Jacob, Ezra, David, Solomon, Job, Joseph, Moses, Aaron, Zachariah, John the Baptist, Jesus, Elias, Elijah, Jonah, Ezekiel (I have given the names as commonly known in the Western world), and also three Islamic prophets, Hud, Shu'ayb and Salih. The final prophet, the culmination of the series of messengers, is Muhammad. Each prophet was suited for his own age —when the time was ripe for revelation —bringing whatever aspect of Divine Truth the Lord thought necessary for man. The role of the prophets was difficult (for they were dealing with obdurate sinners) but they were forceful, intelligent, courageous, honest and truthful, and discharged their messages in full, no matter what obstacles they had to overcome or what penalties they might face. Of these prophets, Muhammad, Noah, Abraham, Moses and Jesus are known in the Qur'an as the People of Determination, and are held in special honor. The prophets received their

Islam is primarily a religion for men. Women play a minor role in it; they are kept in the background. In the mosque they stay behind a screen. When a Muslim sheik opens his tent to friends, his women go into seclusion.

messages for mankind through the medium of Gabriel (or Jibril).

As the prophet immediate to Muhammad, Christ receives a fair amount of attention. Though the Muslims believe that He was born of a virgin and was of an exceptional honor, they do not hold Him to be divine, as Christians do. He is not the Son of God, because "Allah is One, the Eternal God. He begot none, nor was He begotten. None is equal to Him." The Qur'an quotes Jesus as saying, "I am the servant of Allah. He has given me the Gospel and ordained me as a prophet. His blessing is upon me wherever I go, and He has commanded me to be steadfast in prayer and to give alms to the poor as long as I live. He has exhorted me to honor my father and my mother and has purged me of depravity and wickedness. I was blessed on the day I was born, and blessed shall I be on the day of my death; and may peace be upon me on the day when I shall be raised to life." The Qur'an emphasizes that Allah forbade that He Himself should beget a son. Certain Muslims, particularly many of the Sufis, a mystical sect, believe in the Second Coming of Christ, a belief which is condemned by the orthodox.

Since Muhammad superseded and fulfilled the previous prophets in the final act of God's revelation to man, it then follows that all men are Muslims. The following passage from the Traditions (in Arabic, the Hadith or the Apostolic Traditions, a collection of works representing the words and deeds of the

Muslim pilgrims from Turkestan, on their way home from Mecca, stop to pray at a mosque in Damascus.

Prophet and accepted as the second authoritative source after the Qur'an) is one of several to state the theme:

Abu Salamah ibn 'Abd ar-Rayhman was informed that Abu Hurairah said: "The Messenger of God [Muhammad] spoke thus: 'There is no new born child that but belongs naturally to the religion of Islam. It is the parents who make it a Jew or a Christian or a Zoroastrian. Similarly every animal is born complete— have you ever seen one come into the world with its ears cut?'" Then Abu Hurairah recited the verse of the Qur'an which says, "Turn towards the natural religion in which God created men. God's creation cannot be changed. That is the unalterable religion."

This message that all men are born Muslims has in part accounted for Islam's wide-spread acceptance and popularity. Today, as in the past, it is outstripping Christianity in making converts, particularly in Africa and parts of Asia. Of all the world religions Islam has probably had the greatest success in crashing through the barriers of race, color, and nationality. But it is not an easy religion to adhere to, though its teachings may be simply stated. It implies a great measure of individual responsibility. "No soul bears the burden of another," says the Qur'an. This means that each man is fully responsible for his own acts and cannot blame others for his sins and errors. He will be punished or rewarded according to the life he has chosen to lead. Even in the light of his submission to God, his individual responsibility exists: "Whatever good happens to you is from God, whatever evil happens to you is from yourself." "Allah does not change a people's lot unless they change what is in their hearts. If He seeks to inflict misfortune upon men, no one can avert it, because without Him they have no protector."

While I have been talking about "mankind" in a general sense, the Muslim is more likely to think of mankind as male, despite the freedom given women in the Qur'an. Prior to Muhammad, women had no rights in the Arab world, and the Qur'an attempts to alleviate their lot. However, the practical effect of the Qur'an has been to freeze their situation somewhere in the first Islamic century. While Muhammad may have given women an advanced standing in relation to the past, Islamic custom, and even law, have not allowed their natural development. In many Islamic countries women do not even have a minimum of rights; they may be wholly or partially veiled and are often kept in seclusion. A woman is not allowed to have her photograph taken even for a passport (a large X fills the space where the picture would be placed). A woman does not talk to men outside the immediate family, she does not go out alone, and rarely has any civil rights. Her life can be—and often is— hardly more than a long series of servile jobs for the man, from bearing his children (male children are prized) to endless hours in the fields, at the well, the loom and the kitchen, while her husband can and does spend a lot of time at the coffee house and in the mosque. However, the famous Islamic custom which allows a man to have as many as four wives is more talked about than practiced, though I have come across several examples in my travels in the Middle East. One day in the Gaza Strip I was taken to visit a typical refugee family. Only the wife was present, with several small children. "Where is her husband?" I asked my interpreter. The woman replied, rather bitterly, "Oh, he's with his other wife." While working in another Arab country, I had a driver who had four wives and sixteen children and who was quite proud of his family. But this custom tends to be defeated by nature: in the usual course of events there are about an equal number of boy and girl children born, and if a small number of men are going to corner a majority of women in plural marriages, then a large number of men are going to be unmarried and wifeless. However, certain well-off men do make the most of Islamic law, and have the maximum number of wives. In some countries, such as Iran, a man may "marry" widows or relatives or unmarried cousins and thus give them the protection of marriage without treating them, in the literal sense, as wives. However, not all Muslim men can find wives; this shortage leads to the use of prostitutes and to sexual perversion.

 While they play a definitely secondary role in the Islamic world, women are also protected to an extent unknown in the

In India, which has a large Muslim minority, the Shi'ite Muslims celebrate the festival of Muhammad's son-in-law, Ali. The Shi'ites believe that their sect is more orthodox than the Sunnis, who follow a different line of descent from the early khalifs.

West. Within the span of a few days I was twice threatened with death for the same offense, photographing Muslim women. In the first incident, in Somalia, I was attacked by a young shepherd and rescued by a bodyguard, and later in the week, I was seized a group of angry Bedouins and released only after extended negotiations by a United Nations official who spoke Arabic. On another occasion, when I was working with some Jordanian geologists in the countryside above Amman, I wanted to photograph a very charming scene of a young girl washing sheep in a stream. One of my companions (they were all obviously Muslims) told me not to, saying, "She is a woman and is ashamed. She does not want to be photographed because she is a woman, she is very ashamed of being a woman."

There are two main currents in Islam, the Sunnis and the Shi'ites. The divergence stems from the role of the Righteous Khalifs and the question of the orthodoxy of their succession to Muhammad. The Sunnis, who comprise the majority of Muslims, follow the first four khalifs (that is, the Righteously Guided Khalifs) because they had practiced the sunnah, which may be called the traditional usage of the Prophet and his Companions, in their worship and in their acceptance of the Qur'an. The Sunnis split into various divisions over the centuries, due to different interpretations of what they considered the traditional, orthodox doctrine.

The Shi'ites—or Partisans—reject the first three khalifs and follow Ali, Muhammad's son-in-law, who was the fourth khalif, on the theory that he was closer to the Prophet than the intervening khalifs and therefore more orthodox. Shi'ite beliefs run from moderate to radical in the context of orthodox Islam. The more moderate Shi'ites, known as Twelvers, believe that Ali as the Imam, or leader, and his eleven successors, who were also Imams, had not only the correct hereditary succession from Muhammad in both spiritual and temporal spheres, but were also infallible and free from sin. They hold that the twelfth and last Imam disappeared and is in hiding, to return on the day of salvation. The Twelvers were vigorously persecuted by more moderate Muslims, but in the sixteenth century Shi'a became the official version of Islam in Persia. The shahs were said to rule in the name of the Hidden Imam and (in the past) two horses were kept saddled and in readiness for the return of the Mahdi, or Righteous Imam, and for Jesus.

The Mahdi ("The Righteous one of God") apparently comes from Christian influence, Islam in Iraq and Persia being heavily influenced by both orthodox and heretical Christian beliefs, as well as by Zoroastrian and Buddhist doctrines. The Mahdi is the Hidden Imam: he is a spiritual being who will appear at the end of time and restore justice to the world and establish the full power of Islam over

Almsgiving is a common duty of the Muslim, and there are always poor to rely upon the generosity of the good Muslim. This beggar waits outside a mosque in Baghdad.

the ungodly forces that plague mankind. This messianic or eschatalogical belief stems from Christian teaching of the Second Coming of Christ. It has had a great appeal to the Muslim poor, who are all too conscious of the failure of the political and social standards preached by orthodox Islam.

This doctrine of the Mahdi runs throughout Sufism, a very exuberant, wild, and eschatological type of Islamic mysticism which enlivens Shi'a and dates back to the first century of Islam. The term "Sufi" comes from the name of the rough white robes of the poor, as contrasted to the luxurious garments of the Muslim courts. The Sufis voiced a deep, transforming cry that protested against the formalism and worldliness that soon infused Islam. It is a great call for the religion of the heart, expressed in burning, poetic terms that not only included the spoken and written word but music and dancing as well, some Sufis becoming so entranced in their inner visions that they whirled off in ecstatic vibrant dances that left them physically and emotionally exhausted but spiritually one with God. What one finds throughout Sufi mysticism, as in the mysticism of other religions, are images of blinding lights—a light that illumines all souls, a light that burns without burning, a fire that consumes without destroying. In obvious reaction to the harsh surroundings of cramped slums and open glaring deserts there is a yearning for the coolness of the love of the Lord; references to gardens and limpid pools serve as similes for one-

While one man dresses after praying at the Blue Mosque in Jerusalem, another washes his feet. This ritual washing is called wudu.

ness with the Divine. Numerous Sufi brotherhoods sprang up throughout the Muslim world, preaching a mystical love with an intensity that was not only spiritual but physical (sometimes with actual fires and swords), that could destroy the ego in deep meditation, or produce poetry of crystal beauty, or as some of the whirling dervishes did, run wild in an orgy of physical destruction that could end in death for the mystic and the onlookers. In the search for God, the self was to be immolated completely.

We see this immolation of the self in some of the medieval Sufi poets:

He who seeks Me finds Me.
He who finds Me knows Me.
He who knows Me loves Me.
    Him who loves Me I love
    Him whom I love I kill.
    Him whom I kill,
it is I who ransom.
Him whom I have to ransom,
it is I who am his ransom.

My spirit holds You between my skin and
    my bones, if I were to lose You, how
    would I exist?
Your spirit is mingled with mine, like
    water with wine.
So when something touches You, it
    touches me.
Thus I am in everything.
I have become Him whom I love and He
    whom I love has become me.
We are two spirits entwined in one body.
To see me is to see Him, and to see Him
    is to see us.

Between Thou and I is an "It is I" which
   torments me.
By Your "It is I" take away "It is I" from
   between us.
Your image is in my eye, Your name is on
   my lips, Your home is in my heart,
but where then, have You hidden Yourself?

THE MUSLIM WAY OF WORSHIP. Islam
has five major obligations or duties,
known as the Five Pillars. They are: the
Shahadah, or Confession of Faith, the
five daily prayers, the month-long fast
during Ramadan, the giving of alms, and
the pilgrimage to Mecca, if it is at all
possible.

The Shahadah says simply, "I testify
that there is no God but God and that
Muhammad is His Prophet." This is the
basic creed. This is the creed the born
Muslim subscribes to (it is whispered
into his ear immediately after birth) and
that is used as a call to worship and
chanted from the minarets of the
mosques. Converts, of course, must subscribe to it too.

Almsgiving follows a prescribed for-
mula: from two and a half percent of
one's annual income (in either money or
goods) to a tenth of the revenue of certain agricultural products and a fifth of
the income from mines. The alms, known
as zakat, were originally given to the
poor; zakat, which is freely given and
depends on the individual's conscience,
is now donated to the department or
ministry of religion in Muslim countries,
or to mosques and schools in non-Muslim

lands. Fasting is an obligation of the able-bodied during Ramadan, a month which was sacred even before the appearance of Muhammad. The Muslim must abstain from food and drink from dawn (that is, when a man can distinguish between a white and a black thread) to sunset. I have been with Muslims in Bangladesh during Ramadan and found it an inspiring lesson to see how ordinary working men, who lead a hard life even under the best of conditions, spent the day without food or water in extreme heat—cheerfully too, in the spirit that has been enjoined upon them—and then in a kind of joyous celebration broke the fast on the minute when sunset officially came. Then they would take tea and some rice and fruit. A Muslim driver, who was taking me through the Ganges delta, was forced to get up at two or three in the morning and have breakfast then so there would be no chance that he might inadvertently break the fast. He had only a few hours sleep each night—we were working late, too—but he was always lively and cheerful, no matter how hungry he must have been. He never showed any sign of annoyance when I and the other people, who were Hindus and not bound by the fast, had our meals. I suspect now that he felt a certain pride in being able to follow his beliefs so faithfully while the rest of us had such lower standards. This man, Ali, also said his prayers when he had an opportunity, without making a show of them, without embarrassment, and without annoying others.

Prayer is the central act of worship. A

Muslims at prayer: the men (left) are in the Great Mosque in Damascus; the one above is at the Jamah Masjid in New Delhi. The rite is the same wherever one goes.

man's entire life is based on prayer. No Christian monk in a cloistered monastery prays more often than the ordinary Muslim layman and woman. The layman is called to prayer—the Arabic word is salah —five times a day. Salah follows a prescribed ritual, which is rather detailed. The worshipper must first wash, the act of purification being the first of seven obligatory acts. The washing begins with the removal of najasah, which is dirt that may touch the body or the clothes or the place of prayers. Najasah is described as "chiefly what comes from a person or from an animal, like urine or blood. . . . If some of najasah drops into a liquid like oil or a little water, the liquid becomes najasah. If it drops on our body or our clothes or the place of prayers it must be removed. Wine is also najasah." However, milk, sweat and tears are not najasah. Some types of najasah (clear or odorless or tasteless) need be washed only once, but najasah from a dog or a pig must be washed seven times, the first with water mixed with dust.

Hadath must also be removed. Hadath is described as occurring "after one or more of the following matters: Sleeping; the coming out of anything from the lower openings, like urine, wind, and so on; absence of mind because of fainting or being drunk; direct touching of the private parts by the inside of the palm; direct touching between a man and a woman who are not close relatives." So, after urinating or defecating, or after sexual intercourse, or even touching the face or arm of a woman, one has hadath.

However, a man who touches his mother or sister or grandmother in affection does not create hadath.

The removal of hadath is accomplished by a ritual of washing called wudu. The ritual is quite elaborate, beginning with the very thorough washing of the hands (even the dirt under the fingernails is to be removed), and the rinsing of the mouth. The nose is cleaned out. Then the face is completely washed. (Among the prayers that may be said during wudu is one for the face which goes: "God, make my face white on the day of judgment when some are resurrected with white faces and others with black faces.") The forearms, the head, the ears and the ankles are all washed, followed by the recitation of a prayer called the du'a. Hadath has completely gone, and the worshipper is now pure, being able to pray and touch the Qur'an.

This washing is done in the courtyard of the mosque if there is one available to the worshipper. Otherwise he does the best he can, and if water is obviously impossible to get, as in the desert, sand may be used. Each mosque is centered around the fountain in the courtyard; the water must be running. In desert countries this careful washing is a pleasant task, but I have seen Muslims in the mountains of Iran, in winter, washing in water that would be ice if it had not been flowing.

When he prays, the Muslim faces the qiblah, the direction of Mecca. He begins by putting his two hands to his ears and saying, "God is great." Then he places his hands on his chest, the right being over the left, and says a prayer of submission to God, followed by the opening surah, or chapter, Al Fatihah, from the Qur'an. This position is known as the Standing. Still praying, the worshipper puts his hands on his knees so that he is half-bent in a position known as the Bending. He stands again, and then prostrates himself. The toes of both feet, his knees and hands and forehead all must touch the ground as he prays. Now he raises himself to a sitting position with his hands on his knees as he prays for mercy and protection. Another prostration follows and finally he stands again. The entire ritual (called raka'h) is performed twice. The prayers must be said in Arabic if at all possible; most Muslims seem to learn the required prayers for worship though they may learn very little else in Arabic and would be hard put to give a translation. (The Qur'an itself is studied in Arabic, a difficult task for the majority of Muslims since most speak a mother tongue other than Arabic. Translations are rare and not too expert.)

I have dwelt upon the daily ritual of prayer because it is so central to Islam. Though traditionally men may gather in the mosque at noon on Fridays to pray together, there is actually no equivalent of Sunday worship, either Mass or a service or meeting as among Christians, or of the Jewish Sabbath. One worships, alone, every day, five times a day, from childhood, for life. Yet, to the distress of many Muslims, this pattern of prayer is being threatened in the modern world.

Barefoot and totally absorbed, a group of men and a young boy pray to Allah at a Persian mosque.

In the big cities of the Islamic nations the time for prayer is eroding away, and in factories and offices it is increasingly difficult for the pious Muslim to pray as his ancestors did. The time clock and the assembly line demand a submission of their own.

THE HAJI TO MECCA. Each year a million or more Muslims journey to Mecca to fulfill the fifth of the Precepts, the performance of the Haji, or pilgrimage to the sacred Ka'ba of Mecca. Some pilgrims make the trip entirely by foot, walking long miles through Saudi Arabia to Mecca. The most usual route is by ship or plane to Jeddah, the Saudi Arabian port on the Red Sea. At Jeddah (*Pilgrims! Saudi Arabia Welcomes You,* say the signs of Arabic and a dozen other languages), the pilgrim, who might be one of a hundred different nationalities, from Moroccan to Albanian to Syrian to Pakistani, Chinese or Indonesian, changes his normal (often Western) clothes for the simple one-piece unstitched white cotton robe that eliminates the distinction between rich and poor, saint and sinner. He puts on open sandals and usually lets his beard grow. No other garments may be worn, and no jewelry. (In pre-Islamic ages, pilgrims visited the Ka'ba stark naked.) Women, though always completely covered in Islamic countries, change to a white cotton dress, white stockings and gloves, and a scarf over the head. However, a woman removes her traditional veil, because no one may appear before the Ka'ba with a covered face.

Trucks and buses are available for the pilgrim who is unable to walk the fifty miles to Mecca. But most people go by foot along the asphalt walk constructed by King Ibn Saud, feeling that they should approach Mecca as Muhammad did when he returned to demolish the idols of the Ka'ba. The road runs through a flat, featureless plane, surrounded by fine white sand, which changes to low, ore-stained foothills near Mecca. Fourteen miles from the city is a huge sign in Arabic and English, saying: *Stop. Restricted area. Moslems only permitted beyond this point.*

In the past, a few non-Muslims entered Mecca, notably Sir Richard Burton, the nineteenth-century English adventurer, but today it is virtually impossible. Guards armed with submachine guns and walkie-talkies examine everyone's credentials. Beyond this point are a few ruined forts, erected at the time Turkey controlled Arabia and tried to put down the Bedouin tribes, and some pilgrim shelters, one of which was built by Ibn Saud's own hands. The pilgrim is now in the Forbidden Zone, and a great hush falls over the unending procession. Small talk dies away, and the only sounds are the repetition of verses from the Qur'an, repeated over and over like the throbbing of waves breaking on a shore.

The pilgrim goes through a pass in the foothills, and there is Mecca itself, a mass of white buildings nestled among seven hills. Many of the buildings are modern hostels and administrative offices, constructed to handle the crush of pilgrims. The heat is fierce—sometimes as high as 133 degrees—and electric fans have been installed in the arcade surrounding the great square of the Ka'ba. Electric lights burn all night, giving an eerie glare to the sacred structure.

The pilgrim's schedule is full: he is not only expected to circumambulate the Ka'ba seven times (the first three at a run, as Muhammad did when he returned to Mecca) on several occasions and to kiss the Black Stone within it since it is the only surviving relic touched by the hands of the Prophet himself, but also to make a sevenfold circuit (again running part of the way) between two landmarks accepted as the tombs of Hajar and Ismail, to visit a spot called Mina to throw stones at three pillars representing evil spirits, and to pray on Mount Arafat, sacred as the spot where Ibrahim offered Ismail in sacrifice to God, and to sacrifice an animal as Ibrahim had done. These rites, which take several days, are followed by three rather festive days dedicated to a new and more holy life. The pilgrim's head is now shaved. With this he is known as a hajji and may wear the green turban which shows that he has made the pilgrimage to Mecca, an honor which only one out of ten Muslims ever attains. And now he returns to his own land, a man of honor, respect and virtue.

LĀ-ILĀHĀ-ILLĀ-ĀLLĀH *There is no god but God.*

Such are the words which should be the first sounds a Muslim hears at birth, which are the constant refrain of his life. And the words which should be the comfort of his dying breath.

There is no god but God.

CHRISTIANITY

 Go therefore and make disciples of all nations,
baptizing them in the name of the Father,
and of the Son and of the Holy Spirit,
teaching them to observe all that I have commanded you;
and lo, I am with you always,
to the close of the age.

Christ's command, given in various forms in five different places in the New Testament, has been the success of Christianity, and yet, its failure, too. The Roman world accepted Christianity with a great rush, so that by the end of the third century, between an eighth and a quarter of the population was Christian, though it was illegal to be so. When we realize that these conversions were made by individual missionaries who traveled by the simplest means, on foot, or by cart or sailing ship, across a great empire that touched the Atlantic on one edge and Persia on the other, we can only be impressed by the spreading of the seed that took such a deep and steadfast root. The "pagan" world of Rome and Greece was open to the news of Jesus. Eventually all of Europe, from the western islands of

Scandinavia to the eastern-most plains of Russia, had become Christian, along with great sections of the Middle East and North Africa. Conversion was largely peaceful, but force was used from time to time, a notable example being Charlemagne's conversion of the Saxons, whom he had defeated in battle. Yet, while Christianity was spreading across Europe, it virtually disappeared in North Africa and the Middle East when the Muslims swept through the world on their own missions of conversion. The Christian world had always suffered from interior and exterior tensions, ranging from endless battles over doctrine, to actual wars between rival claimants to the Truth that Christ had given the world, to devastating attack by barbarians. By the eleventh century, it experienced a truly horrendous split, the Great Schism of 1054, with Roman Christianity on one side and Greek, or Eastern, on the other. The schism has never been healed; even further schisms were to be the fate of Western Christianity. Nevertheless, despite serious stresses and strains, despite wars and rivalries that could be settled with little short of annihilation, Christianity has shown an amazing vitality and endurance. The Church—that is, Christians of all types—has been written off again and again, but somehow always manages to survive, often battered and weak, and fading away, but in the end getting a new breath and a new life. Christianity experiences a great ebb and flow: Orthodoxy gives way to heresy and schism, and then the chaos begins to flow into reunion and

The Agape, the ancient Christian love feast which was part of the Eucharistic celebration, gradually disappeared as part of the rite. Recently it has been revived in various forms by different Christian churches, but on an unoffficial basis.

ecumenical movements and new understandings, and a wholesale examination of past errors and a restatement of aims, doctrines, values, hopes, aspirations. On the surface nothing remains constant: The Christian world is characterized by a restless energy in which her people seek Christ, reject Him, seek Him again, try to place Him in a new context, take His teachings apart and place them against the surge of their own times. Beneath it, on levels too deep for the average man to seek, there is a solid, unchanging core. Or so the Christian feels and hopes. In one century the nature of Christ sets men against each other, even to the point of death. Just Who is Jesus? Is He man or god or both? Over a millennium later the issue of corruption in the Church splits it savagely with a ferocity that one finds only in wars against barbaric enemies. Yet these were brothers and friends, fathers and sons who fought and killed each other. In our age there is a great reexamination of the past, of lost issues and forgotten causes and seemingly irrelevant arguments and doctrines, in the hope that Christians will again be one. Always there is the attempt to "make the Church relevant," to put it face to face with the nuclear, astronautical, turned-on, freaked-out age that surrounds the Christian wherever he looks.

At the Ascension of Christ into heaven perhaps five hundred men and women believed in Him, but by the time that Peter had finished talking to the crowds of foreign Jews who had come to Jerusalem for the feast of Pentecost, he had converted some three thousand. Within a matter of months most of the cities of the Mediterranean world contained Christian communities. When the Romans destroyed Jerusalem in 70 A.D. the city had fifteen thousand Christians, out of a population of fifty thousand. The Romans dispersed the Jews—and with them the Christians—throughout their empire. This resulted in the establishment of new Christian communities. By the beginning of the fourth century, though Christianity was illegal and Christians were sometimes punished or even executed, the empire contained at least six million Christians in a population of fifty million.

At this point, in the year 312 A.D., an interesting figure appeared to confront the Christian world. This was a Roman general named Constantine, who forms a striking comparison to the Indian emperor Ashoka who had lived six hundred years earlier. The empire was in chaos following the death of Constantine's father, who had been emperor of the western half of the Empire (because of its unwieldy size it was jointly ruled in two administrative areas by co-emperors). Constantine, then eighteen, had asserted his claim to the throne by capturing Gaul, and at twenty-four he was ready to attack the capital city of Rome itself, though he had only twenty thousand troops; his rival and enemy, Maxentius, had a hundred thousand. The night before the battle, Constantine, who was not a Christian, had a dream—as he related later—in which he heard the command to conquer in the name of Christ. He ordered his men to carry the XP, or chi rho, the Greek symbol of Christ, on their shields, though they too were pagan. Constantine won the battle and became emperor of the Roman world. I must add there is a certain ambiguity in Constantine's vision. The XP was also a symbol of the pagan sun god Chronos, and the general's "conversion" could easily have been an afterthought. At any rate, Constantine granted tolerance to Christians (he himself was not baptized until shortly before his death, and he joined one of the heretical sects, the Arians), and the following year, 313 A.D. he confirmed the new standing of Christians with the Edict of Milan.

Constantine's victory was a turning point in the history of Christianity. He had waged the first war in the name of Christ, Chronos aside. From then on Christians had the weight of the state behind them, and war became a recognized means of protecting or establishing the Church. Christ's command to practice love and charity toward one's enemies was set aside; violence was not to be rejected as He had wished. In the past, soldiers turned Christian had preferred to die as martyrs rather than take life (a number of such peace-seekers are still celebrated on the Church calendar), but now war and all its attributes were a part of Christian life and the Christian accepted war and violence as a necessary means of bringing Christ to the world. What might have happened if Constan-

Constantine, the great Byzantine Emperor who granted
toleration to Christianity. This head is a section of a statue,
larger than life size, most of which has been lost.

tine had followed the lesson of Ashoka (whom he could hardly have heard of) is not known but it is an interesting question. By making Christianity the state religion and by throwing the power of the throne behind the Church, the entire direction of Christianity was changed. Once force was accepted by the Church as a valid means of both defense and conversion, it set Christians not only against the "pagan" world but against each other.

But without the eroding pressures of persecution the Christian Church could grow, and did. Within a few centuries most of the Mediterranean area and all of southern Europe was Christian.

Christianity considers itself a fulfillment of Judaism, the messianic prophecy come to life in the person of Jesus Christ, for among the many men who proclaimed themselves the Messiah, only Christ, the Church states clearly and emphatically, is the True Messiah. Whatever the Jews preached, believed in, taught, accepted, was fulfilled in Jesus. The Church is now the Chosen People in all their messianic yearning. It is the New Israel. The Jews, having rejected Christ, are no longer the Chosen People, they are no longer Israel, and now are to be despised and reviled for their failure to see the Truth. Thus the later Christian teaching about the Messiah and the Jews was formed.

And who is this Messiah who splits the world and shakes the universe? He is a "simple" working man, born of a subjugated people. The Gospels tell us something about Him, at least in His final year or two, but almost nothing about His background, and virtually nothing about the social, political and economic conditions of His world. Living conditions were abysmally low. The daily wage for a working man was one denarius, which was the rough equivalent of an American dollar. On this, a man had to support himself and his family. It was an age of messianic hopes, with the daily expectation of the coming of a saviour. (When Christ was ten or twelve a self-proclaimed messiah had appeared among the Jews and when the Romans cut him down, some two thousand of his followers were massacred.)

Palestine was an occupied territory. It was a land held by enemies—the Romans —and ruled by their puppet kings from a dynasty which had been forcibly converted to Judaism within the previous century. The Jews had been in a state of revolt for a long time: There had been the long Maccabean war, a fierce revolt led by a group of very courageous and daring Jewish warriors, and minor revolts and riots, followed by murders and political executions by the Romans and their puppet rulers. When Jesus was born, the current king, the infamous Herod, was known as a ruthless executioner of enemies, whether real or suspected. Later historians wrote that he was believed to be insane.

According to tradition, Jesus began to preach when He was thirty and was crucified at thirty-three. However, it is likely

that His life span may have been longer:
An error by a medieval monk put the
date of His birth in the wrong year. We
know that He was born during the reign
of King Herod, who died sometime before April 12 in what is now counted as
4 B.C. St. Luke says that Jesus was baptized during the reign of Tiberius Caesar,
which would be, by the reckoning of
some experts, 26 or 27 A.D. and by most
others, 28 or even 29 A.D. Jesus was
crucified in 30 A.D. at the earliest. He
was probably between thirty-four and
thirty-six when He died, though a few
experts think He might have been as old
as forty. I make this point about His age
because today we tend to think of Him as
being like a thirty-year-old man. However, in ancient Middle Eastern terms,
and even today in the undeveloped areas
of the world, the majority of people
never outlive their twenties. So, if we try
to think of Jesus in the context of His
times and milieu, He was a wise older
man, definitely mature and experienced
and not the equivalent of a hippie activist.

Our knowledge of Jesus comes primarily from the Four Gospels, plus scattered references in the Acts of the
Apostles and the Epistles, and in certain
now-obscure Christian works which have
no canonical standing; there are also two
or three very brief and indirect references
to Him in Roman documents which add
no details but at least give objective
proof that He existed, a fact which has
been challenged from time to time by
skeptics.

It may have been the fear of being

A priest carries the Eucharist in a procession on the Aran
Islands in Ireland's Galway Bay.

thought irreverent or impious that has led to a rather negative and passive picture of Jesus in the Western part of the Church. He invariably comes across in drawings, sermons, literature, and religious works as a sweet, pious, almost effeminate figure with long hair and a wispy beard. But he could hardly have fitted the traditional saccharine portrait. He sounds like a man with a lot of energy, and a commanding presence, outspoken and forceful. When He walked people ran to keep up with Him. He seems to have been physically tough; aside from the hard living conditions, He experienced annihilating torture without cracking. There are certain indications of humor (though one does not normally think of the Son of God making jokes), but in those hard times He must have had a lot of "personality," charisma, style—whatever you want to call it—to have such a profound effect upon people who had already seen enough of peasant revolts, false prophets, traitors, and felt the weight of a foreign army.

About Jesus Himself there have been a wide variety of opinions, though the Church (and later the State) tried to hold to uniformity. The traditional view, evolved during years of discussions, councils, arguments with heretics, theological speculation, deep prayer, and mystical insight is that He was truly the Son of God, and was both God and man, the belief formulated by the Council of Nicea in 325. Jesus was stated to be "conceived by the Holy Spirit" and "consubstantial with the Father," two phrases which state

In an ecumenical celebration, two prelates, one Roman Catholic, the other Episcopalian, embrace each other. After some four hundred years of major schisms, the Christian churches are beginning to meet, not only to hold services but even to unite.

the mystery of the Trinity in terms which have been subscribed to by the majority of Christians, particularly Roman Catholics, Eastern Orthodox, and many Protestants. Yet groups of Christians refused to accept these definitions, and for centuries religious wars rent the Christian world, some people seeing Christ only as a spirit, others only as God, or only as man, or even merely as a kind of religious genius. Some people saw Him as a man who was favored with some special kind of relationship with God and nothing more, while others could accept Him without God, or any god at all, in the picture.

But Christ, both God and man, is part of a mystery which the Church can only state and which the Christian must accept on faith, being unable to prove with finality in rational arguments. This mystery is that Christ is one member of a Trinity, the other members being the Father and the Holy Spirit (or Holy Ghost). The idea of a Trinity is anathema to both Jews and Muslims, who see God only as One. The mystery of Christ is further compounded in the doctrine of the Eucharist, which states that Christ offered Himself to all mankind, in the form of bread and wine, at the Last Supper, the Passover meal he shared with his followers. In the most traditional and orthodox Christian belief, shared by Roman Catholics, Eastern Orthodox, and certain Protestant sects, this offering is literally Christ's Body and Blood, seen by human eyes in the form of bread and wine. The doctrine is central to the traditional churches, though their theologians may state it in various ways; the reform churches accept the teaching as symbolic and not literal.

Jesus left a confused group of men behind him when He died. They were not too sure of the Resurrection, but were convinced by the empty tomb, and in the case of Thomas, by Jesus exhibiting His wounds. What is remarkable from that point on is that Christianity spread with such explosive force, from one end of the Roman Empire to the other, but by largely peaceful means. At first the missionaries worked within the Jewish communities (Christians and Jews did not fully drift apart for several centuries), getting Jews to accept Christ. The early converts remained Jews, however, and converts from the pagan world had to become Jews in the fullest sense of the word to be Christian, undergoing circumcision and following Jewish ritual and law. But the conversion of large numbers of pagans to the Judaeo-Christian sect within Judaism brought problems of many kinds, and after the Apostles had hammered out the answer in a very acrimonious debate in Jerusalem, in what is sometimes counted as the First Ecumenical Council, it was decided that converts need not become Jews but were to be taken in without undergoing circumcision or submitting to Jewish law. When the Jews revolted against the Romans in 70 A.D. the Christian community refused to participate. Nor did they participate in the final great

A Jesuit scholar, with the aid of infra-red light and special glasses, reads an ancient, faded almost illegible Nestorian manuscript. Modern techniques are helping to add to the knowledge of earlier Christianity.

Jewish rebellion against the Romans in 132–135 A.D. led by Bar Kochba who was believed by a number of his followers to be the Messiah; the Christians had already accepted Christ as the Messiah and to them Bar Kochba was an impostor. Judaism and Christianity were becoming two different religions.

Before Constantine, Christians had begged for relief from persecution and for the right to practice their religion without interference. After the emperor had issued the Decree of Toleration, putting the Church on a near-official basis, Christianity's demands grew stronger. As the Church and throne became more and more entwined in a commitment that was seen as supernatural (the emperor of the Eastern half of the empire was regarded as a kind of Christ on earth, a doctrine that the Western kings also assumed later), the Church felt sufficiently strong to demand that those who did not agree with it should either be forced into agreement or persecuted, even to death. Heretical beliefs—those which did not conform to the beliefs of the majority of bishops (usually expressed in ecumenical or "world" councils)—continued to plague the Church for centuries and were ruthlessly put down whenever possible.

Since the Roman Empire was ruled in two sections, two major Christian traditions developed, one centered on the emperor in Constantinople and the other on the chief bishop of Rome, the Pope. The Eastern and Western Churches were,

in theory, a single church, but there were long periods in which they were opposed to each other on various matters ranging from theological doctrines to ritual practices. The split began to harden as the popes began to assert themselves as the primary authority over all Christians, on the basis that they were the successors to Saint Peter, to whom Christ had given the honor of being "the Rock upon which I found my Church." A final rupture came in the eleventh century and has continued to the present, each great branch considering itself unique and the only True Church. But with the break of 1054 A.D. the tragedy of Christian disunion was only beginning: the papacy, which tried to enforce more and more stringent control, found itself faced with a major protest. culminating in the great reform movement of the sixteenth century. Roman Catholicism, which had survived the Dark Ages of Western Europe and flowered in the great golden period of the twelfth and thirteenth centuries, suffered a series of attacks from all quarters, from theologians and intellectuals, peasants and kings in revolt, reformers, and protesters. This spontaneous uprising throughout Europe, sparked by arguments over doctrine and abuses within the Church (such as the selling of indulgences, which it was believed would free a soul from the sufferings of Purgatory, and the tremendous corruption of much of the clergy and the papal court) split Western Christianity into such antagonistic sects that it has never recovered. National churches arose, united

Daily and several times on Fridays, pilgrims follow the Way of the Cross said to have been taken by Jesus through the streets of Jerusalem.

In southern India a monk belonging to the Syro-Malabar rite, believed to have been introduced to the Cochin coast in the third century, prays in the same manner one sees in paintings of ancient Christians in the catacombs.

only by their common opposition to Roman Catholicism. The papacy could not contain the protests, which ran from new interpretations of traditional teaching, unauthorized and "heretical" translations of the Bible, to quite legitimate objections to corruption on all levels of the Church. In Germany, Bohemia, Switzerland, France, England, and Italy the Church was split into fragments, the tragedy being compounded by the fact that soon the Protestants fought among themselves and new sects were founded. By the end of the sixteenth century, at a time when Western man was in a great intellectual, political, and economic renaissance and the whole world was being explored, European Christendom was hopelessly shattered. Catholicism and Protestantism found each other in grievous error, and each church or sect and all its successors and offspring saw themselves as the One True Church. Each was unique and "chosen," the others being incomplete, erroneous, and heretical. Christianity had reached the point where not only were non-Christians to be excluded, but also Christians of other sects. The enemy was everywhere. Thus, in the great missionary ventures, a convert from Hinduism to Catholicism was still a man in error for the Presbyterian, and a convert from Buddhism to Methodism was not a full Christian according to the Catholic. It has not been until the past few decades that attempts to heal these multitudinous ruptures have had any success. It took years for members of the various Protestant churches to even *talk* to each other in an understanding and open manner. There have been a few reunions of churches, but the major difficulty—I won't call it an obstacle—is the insistence of the Roman Catholic Church that true reunion and complete unity of the Christian world can be achieved only by the submission of all Christians to its authority, since it sees itself as the True Church alone and the repository of Christian truth.

Christianity is a world religion, and so proclaims herself. Christianity is also an exclusive religion, born of an exclusive religion, Judaism, and cousin (or even brother) to another, Islam. One can be either Jew or Christian or Muslim, but not two or all three. However, a man can be a Hindu and a Buddhist, if he so wishes, or even a Hindu and a Christian, though no Christian would accept the combination.

This dichotomy presents grave difficulties to the Christian, since he has been taught since childhood that "the gospel must first be preached to all nations" and enjoined to "Go therefore and make disciples of all nations." Even if the Christian cannot do this personally, he usually supports his own missions in the field, that is, he supports the missionary efforts of his own denomination and not those of others.

Missionaries like to speak of the potential "harvest for Christ." (Yet these same people would be most resentful if a Hindu saw America in terms of a potential "harvest for Krishna.") Having at one point worked in the religious field, and having traveled extensively in the areas of these future "harvests," I have given the situation some thought; it finally occurred to me that Christianity is, despite its world-wide claims, a Western religion. That is, it is primarily a white man's religion. The black, yellow, and brown members of the Christian churches form a very small minority. Accurate figures are not available, and such figures would be suspect anyway, but perhaps 5 percent of the world's Christians have skins other than white—that is, they are people of Asia, Africa, and large areas of Latin America and the West Indies. When Christian missionaries began to penetrate the parts of the world which were being opened up by the colonizing powers in the sixteenth and seventeenth centuries, they made a few converts but in general met with either indifference or hostility. Out of perhaps 600 million people in India only about 10 million are Christian, and some of them were converted as early as the third century. Islam, a relative latecomer to the Indian subcontinent, had a markedly greater success, so that today about 180 million people out of the 720 million that comprise India, Pakistan, and Bangladesh are Muslim. The number of Christians in the other Asian lands, in Japan, China, Indonesia, and so on, is very small. The Buddhist nations have not surrendered to Christianity, though substantial numbers of Buddhists have become Muslim. In Mediterranean Africa, Christianity quickly fell before the Muslim forces. The churches have had the greatest successes in black Africa, but again the Muslims are now reported making a tremendous number of converts from among both the "pagan" population and the Christians. In Latin America, which is ostensibly Christian (and mainly Roman Catholic), the churches have a slim hold and are, in the nations which are heavily Indian or black, still trying to purify Christianity of "pagan" practices and beliefs. Something like 80 percent of the Roman Catholic clergy in Latin America is foreign, and some countries have never had an indigenous vocation to the priesthood. This is true even after four centuries of Catholic missionary activity.

Not only is it an axiom of faith that the world must be converted to Christianity, it must be converted to a special type of Christianity. The result is that, to give but two examples, we find Roman Catholic missionaries in the American south working to convert Protestants to Catholicism, and Protestant missionaries in Latin America attempting to convert Catholics to their particular denomination. However, the primary goal of all the Christian churches is to convert the non-Christian. Considering the amount of energy, money, and time being spent, a stupendous effort is being made without more than a token sign of success. And why is that? The members of other religions can usually accept Jesus without difficulty, but they cannot accept Christianity. Sister Nivedita, an Irish woman who became a Hindu, remarked that

In many parts of the former colonial world, the Christian churches are making serious efforts to identify with traditional forms of worship instead of forcing western types upon the people. Here a community of Indian Christians wears Indian clothing, sits upon the floor while worshipping as Hindus do, and even practices yogic meditation.

Christianity in India "carries drunkenness in its wake—for if you teach a man what he has thought right is wrong, he is likely to think that what he has thought wrong is right." Ananda Coomaraswamy, a Hindu, has written: "Your 'Christian' civilization is ending in disaster—and you are bold enough to offer it to others!" He points out that there are many very learned Christians "whose real knowledge of any other religion but their own is virtually nil, because they have never imagined what it might be to *live* these other faiths"; he concludes: "There are many paths that lead to the summit of one and the same mountain; their differences will be more apparent the lower down we are, but they vanish at the peak; each will naturally take the one that starts from the point at which he finds himself; he who goes round about the mountain looking for another is not climbing. Never let us approach another believer to ask him to become 'one of us,' but approach him with respect as one who is already 'one of His,' who *is*, and from whose invariable beauty all contingent being depends!"

There are vast psychological differences (as well as theological, cultural, and practical differences) which separate Christianity from the other religions of the world. Sarvepalli Radhakrishnan, a Hindu, says:

While the East believes that there are realities which cannot be clearly seen, and even assumes that logical attempts to formulate them in communicable

*propositions do violence to them, the
West [that is, the Christian world] demands clearness and is shy of mystery.
. . . There is an anxiety for definition and
form in the Western religions.*

D. T. Suzuki, a well-known Japanese Zen
Buddhist, wrote:

*Christian symbolism has much to do with
the suffering of man. The crucifixion is
the climax of all suffering. Buddhists also
speak much about suffering and its climax is the Buddha serenely sitting under
the Bodhi tree by the river Niranja. Christ
carries his suffering to the end of his
earthly life whereas Buddha puts an end
to it while living and afterward goes on
preaching the gospel of enlightenment
until he quietly passes away under the
twin Sala trees. . . . Christ hangs helpless,
full of sadness on the vertically erected
cross. To the Oriental mind, the sight is
almost unbearable. . . . The crucified
Christ is a terrible sight.*

The Buddhist cannot comprehend this
central Christian symbol. What is also
distasteful is "the symbolism of eating the
flesh and drinking the blood [of Christ,
in the Eucharist]. To non-Christians, the
very thought of drinking the blood is
distasteful." To Suzuki the essential difference may be summarized in this comparison:

*"Christianity has something in it which
stirs, agitates, and disturbs. Being combative and exclusive, Christianity tends to*

wield an autocratic and sometimes domineering power over others, in spite of its claim to democracy and universal brotherhood. . . . Buddhism is a religion of peace, serenity, equanimity, and equilibrium. It refuses to be combative and exclusive. On the contrary, it espouses broadmindedness, universal tolerance, and aloofness from world discrimination."

Another Japanese Buddhist, Fumio Masutani, puts the difference in other terms:

Buddha has taught that we should depend on ourselves and the dharma as refuge, and on nothing else. In Christianity, the spirit of self-reliance and the desire for reasoning are to be abandoned; the flower of faith is to bloom through faith in Jesus. Buddhism upholds reason and urges us to develop it, Christianity denounces human reason and exhorts us to be saved by God in humble consciousness of our sin.

I could give numerous examples of the psychological gulf but I think the reader grasps the basic problem. However, Jesus Himself is not always the stumbling block. Radhakrishnan has said:

There are human beings with extraordinary, original powers and entrusted with Divine commissions. Being heirs of Divine powers and glories, they form a class of their own. To this class belong the Incarnations of God like Christ,

Krishna, Buddha . . . and their devotees [saints] of the highest order. . . . The saviours of humanity are those who seek God, and being at the same time anxious to share their happiness of divine vision with others, they willingly undergo the troubles of rebirth in the world in order to teach and lead on struggling humanity to its goal.

An Avatara [incarnation] is a human messenger of God, He is like a viceroy of the mighty Monarch. As when there is any disturbance in some far off province, the king sends the viceroy to quell it, as whenever there is any waning of religion in any part of the world, God sends his Avatara there to guard virtue and foster its growth.

When a mighty log of wood floats down the stream, it carries on it hundreds of birds and does not sink. . . . So when a Saviour incarnates, innumerable are the men who find salvation by taking refuge in him.

The Avatara solves the most difficult and intricate problems of life and the soul as the simplest things in the world, and his expositions are such as a child can follow. He is the sum of Divine knowledge, whose light dispels the accumulated ignorance of ages.

A Hindu, Swami Akhilananda, who was a member of the Ramakrishna Order, a Hindu missionary movement, and who lived in America for many years, speaks of Jesus as a divine incarnation. He quotes St. John: "The Word was made flesh and

Guatemalan peasants, according to their custom, sit on the floor of their church as Mass is celebrated.

dwelt among us." This is a concept which presents no difficulty for the Hindu. "There seems to be a marked difference between the personalities known as divine incarnations and other, ordinary people," says the Swami. "Incarnations of God are fully aware of their purpose, goal, and method of Life. . . . From the Hindu point of view, Jesus was fully aware of His mission as an incarnation. . . . Christianity and Hinduism are the two great religions which accept the fact that there have been numerous incarnations in the history of the world, of whom Jesus was one, while the Christians take Jesus to be the only one."

The Swami says about incarnations:

They radiate so much joy that even a disturbed and disgruntled person becomes peaceful and restful after contact . . . Divine incarnations are of course eternally free and they not only transform human beings by giving them illuminations but they also start new civilizations.

Mahatma Gandhi, who spent many years with Christians and had read widely in Christian works, including the Bible, could not accept Jesus even on the basis of his being an avatar:

It was more than I could believe that Jesus was the only incarnate son of God, and that only he who believed in Him would have everlasting life. If God could have sons, then all of us were His sons. If Jesus was like God, or God Himself, then all men were like God and could be God Himself.

What concerns Christians is that not only does the rest of the world *not* accept Christ, but that if they do, they accept Him on their terms, not on those of the missionaries. After the success of the first few centuries, there have been, relatively speaking, few new converts. The growth of Christianity has come from the natural increase of population. The "world" has not been converted nor, as the Jewish theologian Martin Buber points out, has it been redeemed. What then is the problem? I remember talking to a fundamentalist Protestant missionary who had spent fifteen years in India. He felt he was making no progress at all, and his frustrations were directed against not only Hindus but Roman Catholics. I recall that he denounced the "cult" of statues among both. However, his frustrations went beyond that: He was working hard with the people in his area, he had given them a school and hospital services, and held religious classes for them, but conversions were few, being mainly from other Christian groups. He said, "I don't know what the Lord wants of *me*. We are doing our best but things seem to be getting worse." This, in many mission areas, is the inevitable report. A French missionary, Father Charles de Foucauld, spent most of his adult life in the Sahara in an attempt to convert the Muslim nomads, and at the time of his death—he was murdered by some Taureg warriors—he had made only one convert, an old woman.

Christians talk of the seed being planted, yet why hasn't the seed sprouted in Asia and Africa, to say nothing of "Christian" Latin America, as it did once in Europe?

I think one of the main problems is the Westerner's failure to see other people as people. He tends to look upon people outside his own sphere of interest as "souls" if he is a missionary, "bodies" if he is a soldier, a "market" if he is a businessman, and as "natives" in general. My files contain several damning and embarrassing statements by Westerners—in this case missionaries—which reflect the general attitude toward the rest of the world. A mission magazine talks of the "chains of paganism" in referring to Hinduism, showing a complete ignorance of the Hindu view of God; on another page it makes fun of Eskimos' inability to speak English properly; in an article about the heroic work of another missionary in India it calls Hindus who opposed conversion "oppressors" and "scoundrels"—these are people who saw their religion, their culture and the very fabric of their social structure threatened by a foreigner. In an article on Muslims—erroneously called "Mohammedans"—the writer speaks of the difficulties of making converts, one being "a certain almost innate fanaticism which makes a propagandist out of every adult Moslem"; however, says the writer, "There is a break in the wall of opposition." Western ideas are gaining entrance and "Young Mohammedans are returning to their countries after a European education and have lost their respect for the Koran, formerly held as sacred as the Bible." In a reference to Hinduism the article says: "The average educated Hindu is daily hardening himself against the influence of Christianity. The ignorant pagan clings superstitiously to the religion of his ancestors."

On a more sophisticated level, a Christian missionary who has become an Indian citizen in order to be closer to his people has written: "The trouble is that for the Hindu mind the experience of God has been so overwhelming that it is difficult for it to affirm the reality of the world"—"Hindu philosophy," he explains, "starts from *the experience of the reality of God*," and by some twist in logic which is hard to follow he then concludes that "the Hindu mind needs to discover Christ," as if the Hindu were in error in beginning with the Ultimate.

For its entire history the Church has worked for the conversion of the Jews. In its Good Friday liturgy, the Roman Catholic Church made a special point of praying for the "perfidious Jews" (pro perfidis Judeis), "That our God and Lord will remove the veil from their hearts, so that they too may acknowledge our Lord Jesus Christ." This was the one passage where the faithful did not kneel, though they knelt when they prayed for heretics, schismatics, and pagans. This passage was altered by Pope John XXIII, but the sentiment remains, and the Second Coming of Christ is intimately connected with the expected conversion of the Jews. In the past when conversion by persuasion

Christian revival takes many forms. Not only are there "forward" movements such as folk and rock services and Masses, but there is also a return in some cases to earlier, simpler forms. This is a "primitive" Benedictine monastery in New Mexico which seeks to find the simplicity of early monastic life.

failed, then conversion by force was tried by Christians, with understandably lamentable results. Why haven't the Jews been converted, when day in and day out the Church has preached that the Messiah, so long awaited by Israel, had indeed arrived?

The Christian church in all its branches has ascribed the failure of the Jews to accept Jesus as Messiah, roughly, to obstinacy, and has treated this obstinacy roughly. To be a Jew in the Christian world has been to be a man without rights, a man despised, a man hated. The Jews have been face to face with the Messiah longer than any other people, through their prophets, but especially through their Christian neighbors, rulers, oppressors, murderers, for the entire period since Christ's death. Of all the people who are not Christian, the Jews, perhaps, know Jesus better than any other, because He was a Jew, lived, thought, worked, died as a Jew at the hands of aliens who cared nothing for Jews, as Jews were thenceforth to die at the hands of others who cared nothing for Jews except as a target of conversion.

Christianity lives or falls on the basis that Jesus is the Messiah proclaimed by the Old Testament and that He was truly the Son of God, sent to redeem all mankind. But, say the Jews (along with the Muslims) this view of Jesus is an error which began with Saint Paul. There has been extensive thinking by Jews on the problem of Jesus, which has been summarized succinctly by a contemporary American Jewish writer, Arthur A. Cohen:

"Paul takes Israel seriously, but it is an Israel in which no Jew believed. The Israel of Paul is a theological construction. . . . Such a use of the presence of Israel cannot be less than a falsehood in our sight." The Christian view that the theme of the Old Testament is Christ and only Christ, a view expounded by Paul (and subsequently by the Church), is received by Jews with "uncomprehending anger or amazement."

Not only have the mass of the Jewish people rejected all the messiahs who presented themselves to Israel throughout history, but they have rejected Jesus, the one messiah who has been accepted by large numbers of non-Jews. The Jews cannot accept Jesus as the Son of God because, as Cohen writes, Israel "knows from its birth only a single God, to multiply and proliferate him is not only a stumbling block but a meaningless unreality. A messiah to be sure; a Son of God, hopeless!" Cohen also says: "It is . . . for me, a Jew, as much of a mystery that Christianity survived and triumphed as it is a mystery for Christianity that the unconverted Jew persists, not only in his unbelief but in the confident assertion that he is still chosen by God, covenanted to him, and patient before his ultimate decision." For the average Jew, Christ "was paid little attention by the Jews of his day; and, given the unremitting efforts of Christendom for two millennia to enforce the attention of the Jew, it must be remarkable and disconcerting to Christian missionaries to observe how little attention he is paid by Jews even today." But the unbelief of Israel in Jesus as messiah is not unbelief in God. The Jew "is saved by God himself, being with him from his own birth." Israel was with God from the beginning and will be with Him to the end.

In contrast to the Church, which sees the conversion of the Jews as proof of her own Truth, the Jews see the situation reversed: "There is still no peace—even more, that there is no *shlamut,* no perfection until Christianity is reunited with Israel, until it has learned to transcend the Son to the Father, until it too shall have learned to say Lord and Lord alone, having been instructed to do so by the Son."

Cohen concludes: "We patiently await the return of Christendom to the Synagogue, as we patiently await the coming of the messianic herald of the End. . . . Can we be more than patient before the reunion? What more has Israel to offer the world than eternal patience?"

The Muslims see Christianity in much the same manner, as a people in serious error, though Christ is honored as a prophet, as a man of special sanctity, but not as God nor the Son of God. "The conception that God should have issue is viewed with a feeling akin to horror," wrote a Bengali Muslim, Maulavi Saiyid Amir Ali, adding that "Muslims do not recognize that modern Christianity, overladen with Greek philosophy and Pauline mysticism, represents the true religion Jesus in fact taught. They consider that Islam represents true Christianity." Amir Ali states that Muslims believe that the

Christian Gospels were tampered with and garbled, giving an imperfect and erroneous view of the life and preachings of Jesus. " 'God is one God, there is no God but God' and the Muslim expression of faith does not allow for Jesus."

Few people of other religions dispute that Jesus was a great teacher and holy man. A number of people can even see Him as a form of God, as do some Hindus, or as a divinely chosen prophet, as do Muslims. What Jesus taught, aside from a few teachings which non-Christians believe were added by others, is easily accepted. There is a tremendous lack of comprehension in the thinking of Christendom. It cannot understand why the rest of the world does not accept Christianity as easily as it accepts its other gifts, the jet plane, the motorcycle, the printing press, the motion picture, the truly magnificent concepts of democracy, general education, a parliamentary system, charity for the poor and disadvantaged, modern medicine, and so on. Yet the world is not easily impressed by Christianity in action, for most of it has been enslaved —literally, economically, socially, psychologically—by Christendom, and the discrepancy between Christian teachings and Christian practices is too great to overcome. Even the form in which Christianity is preached in Asia, Africa, and the Indies is incredible if not ludicrous: an odd-colored man in funny clothes, perspiring, with a flushed face, speaking the language badly or not at all, wanting his hearers to abandon everything they hold sacred, their traditional beliefs, their cul-

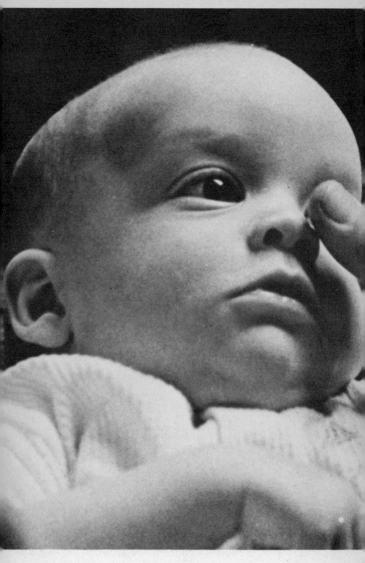

With each baptism the Church renews herself.

ture, institutions, even their families, to subscribe to a doctrine that his fellow whites barely pay lip service to.

I won't push the subject further. If Christianity is to be truly Christian, then Christians will have to become Christian. Mahatma Gandhi put the problem quite succinctly when he stated a fact known all over the world by "native" peoples:

I have always felt that mission work will be the richer if missionaries accept as settled facts the faiths of the people they come to serve—faiths which, however crude, are valuable to them. . . . Missionaries who come to India are laboring under a double fallacy: that what they think best for another person is really so, and that what they think best for themselves is best for the whole world. I am pleading for a little humility. . . . The kink is in the Church thinking that there are people in whom certain things are lacking, and that you must supply them whether they want them or not.

Gandhi asks Christians to return to the teachings of Jesus. "Jesus preached not a new religion but a new life." He suggests that "there should be less of theology and more of truth" in all that Christians say and do:

I have two good Christian friends who gave up theology and decided to live the Gospel of Christ. . . . Spiritual life has greater potency than radio waves. When there is no medium between me and my Lord, and I simply become a willing ves-

sel of His influence to flow into it, then I overflow the water of the Ganges at its source. There is no desire to speak when one lives the truth. Truth is the most economical of words.

INDEX

A

Aaron, 170
Abbasids, 167
  decline of, 169
  Islamic culture and, 167–169
Abhidhamma Pitak, 69
Abraham, 170. See also Abram; Ibra-
    him
  ascent to Heaven of, 140
  Canaan given to, 109, 114
  God's Covenant and, 12, 105, 109
  sacrifice of Isaac and, 108–109, 120
  trek of, 106–108
Abram, 105, 106
Absolom, 120
Abu Bakr, 166–167
Abu Hurairah, 173
Abu Salamah ibn 'Abd
    ar-Rayhman, 173
Abyssinia, 155
Acts of the Apostles, 204
Adam, 170
  Arab tradition about, 155
Afghanistan, 52
Africa. See also North Africa
  Christianity in, 216, 225
Ahab, 122
Alexandria (Egypt), 124
Ali (Muhammad's son-in-law), 178.
    See also ben Abu Talib, Ali
Allah, 154, 156, 172. See also Islam,
    concept of God in
Allah, Khalifat Rasul, 166–167
Almsgiving
  in Islam, 183
Amir Ali, Maulavi Saiyid, 230
Amman (Jordan), 177
Amos, 123
Anagamai, 89
Ananda, 81
Anandamayi Ma, 22
Angel Gabriel, 153. See also Jibril
Angel Jibril, 153. See also Jibril
Angels. See also Jibril
  appearance to Uruvela of, 66
  at Buddha's birth, 58
Animism
  Hinduism and, 27–28
  Islam and, 154, 165
Apostles, 208
Apostolic traditions, 172
Arabia, 108, 153, 155, 158
  civil disturbances in, 166, 167
  submission to Islam of, 165

Arabic, 188
Arabs
  Holy Land and, 118
  Ismael as founder of, 106
  modern Israel and, 147
Arafat, Mount, 191
Arahat, 86
Aramaic, 128
Arhat, 91
Arians, 200
Arjuna, 27, 34
Ark
  of King David, 120–121
Armenia, 92
Artha, 21
Aryans, 14, 15, 19
Ascension of Christ, 198
Asceticism, 4
  in Buddhism, 33
  in Hinduism, 22–23, 28
  in Jewish mysticism, 142
Ashram, 23
Ashoka, 51, 199, 202
  pillars, memorial, of, 52
Asia
  Christianity in, 215, 216–218, 225,
    226
  spread of Islam to, 165
Assimilation
  Judaism and, 145, 147
Assyrians, 14, 124
Astrology
  Hinduism and, 33
Atheism, 4
Atman, 24
Autobiography of a Yogi, 22
Avatara, 221, 223

B

Baal Shem Tov, 142–143
Baba, Meher, 23
Babylon, 127
Babylonians, 14
Babylonian Exile, 124
Baghdad (Iraq), 155
Bahai, 3
Bangladesh, 39, 185
  Islam in, 215
Baptism
  of Constantine, 200–202
  of Jesus, 204
Barbarians, 132
Bar Kochba, 209

Basket of Discipline, 90
Basket of Discourses, 90
Basket of Ultimate Doctrine, 90
Basrah, 163
Beat Generation, 93
Bedouin, 163, 177, 190
Beggars. See also Almsgiving
  as Hindu holy men, 63, 65
ben Abu Talib, Ali, 167, 178
ben Arach, Rabbi Eliezer, 140
Benares, 8, 71
  as sacred center, 39, 41, 71
Bending, the, 188
Benevolence
  of God, 2
Bengal, Bay of, 38
ben Hananya, Rabbi Joshua, 112–113
ben Uziel, Rabbi Jonathan, 140
ben Zakkai, Jochanan, 131, 140
Bethel
  mountain of, 106
Bhagavad Gita, 24, 27, 34, 35
Bhagavata Purana, 35
Bhakti, 30, 35
Bhikkhus, 23, 60
Bhutan, 102
Bible, 34, 46, 110, 114, 118, 233, 226
  New Testament of, 170
  Old Testament of, 170
Bishops, 209
Black Stone
  of the Ka'ba, 156, 191
Blinding lights
  as Sufic images, 181
Bodhidharma, 98–99
Bodhisattva, 66, 92, 93
Bodhi tree, 52, 219
Book of Creation, 142
Brahma, 7, 17, 39
Brahmans, 9, 33, 34, 36, 41, 47, 66, 71,
  83
Branch, the, 126
British
  in Palestine, 131, 145
Brooklyn, New York
  Hasidim in, 143
Buber, Martin, 110–111, 118, 224
Buddha, 12. See also Buddha, Gau-
  tama; Buddha, Lord Gautama
"Buddha" (Enlightened One), 55, 62,
  83, 101
Buddhahood, 54, 65, 66, 69, 83, 101.
  See also Enlightenment
  Four Signs of, 58–59
Buddha, Gautama, 12, 33, 52, 54, 219,
  221
  birth of, 54, 55, 58
  death of, 80–81, 219
  early years of, 55, 59
  family of, 57
  marriage of, 59

myths about, 81–82, 83
reincarnations of, 57
search for Buddhahood of, 62, 63–
  66
teachings of, 54, 71, 73, 75–77, 78,
  80, 83, 84, 85, 89–91, 220
Zen and, 93, 95
Buddha, Lord Gautama, 8, 51–52. See
  also Buddha, Gautama
Buddhism, 1, 8, 51–103. See also
  Buddha, Gautama, teachings
  of; Tantric Buddhism; Zen
  Buddhism
  Christianity compared with, 219–
  220
  concept of God absent in, 84–85
  conversion to, 52
  decline in India of, 102
  Five Supernatural Powers of, 87, 89
  influence on other religions of,
  16, 92, 101–102, 178
  Northern School of, 91
  practicality of, 84
  revival, Asian, of, 102
  Southern School of, 91
  spread of, 52, 90–91, 101–103
Burma
  spread of Buddhism in, 91, 102
Burton, Sir Richard, 190

C

Calendar, Muslim, 161
Canaan, 105, 106, 108, 109, 114, 116.
  See also Promised Land
  conquest by Israelites of, 118–119
  given to Abraham, 105, 109, 114
  seven nations of, 118
Caste system, 4, 17, 19, 36
  conversion to Christianity and, 46
  conversion to Islam and, 45–46
  Hinduism and, 17, 45–48
  origins of, 19–20
  technology, modern, and, 47–48
Catholicism, 46, 211, 213. See also
  Roman Catholicism; Western
  Christianity
Causality
  meditation by Buddha on, 71
Celibate life. See also Monasticism
  denial of, in Judaism, 137
Ceylon, 52
  spread of Buddhism in, 91
Chain of Causation, 69
Chaldeans, 124
Ch'an, 87, 96
Channa, 63
Chariot mysticism, 140
Charity
  in Judaism, 138–139

China, 162
    Buddhism in, 90, 91, 98, 165
    Christianity in, 215
Chinese, 93
Chi rho
    as symbol of Christ, 200
Chosen People, 109–111, 122, 136
    Christian concept of, 202
Christ, 9, 11, 12, 54, 196, 198, 219.
        See also Jesus
    Body and Blood of, 207
    crucifixion of, 219
    Islamic concept of, 172, 230–231
    as Messiah, 202–203, 209, 228–230
    Resurrection of, 208
    teachings of. See Jesus, teachings
        of
Christianity, 3, 4, 27, 112, 195–234.
        See also Eastern Christianity;
        Western Christianity
    in Asia, 215
    Buddhist influences on, 16
    compared with Buddhism, 219–220
    concept of Messiah in, 202–203, 209
    division of, 196, 209, 211. See also
        Eastern Church; Western
        Church
    as exclusive religion, 214
    faith in, 220
    influence on Islam of, 178, 181
    Jews and, 132–133, 135, 202, 208,
        226, 228
    reform movements in, 211
    spread of, 52, 195, 198–200, 208
    supernatural aspects of, 209
    teachings of, 220. See also Jesus,
        teachings of
Christians, 110, 154, 155. See also
        Christianity
Chronos, 200
Church (Christian), the, 196, 198, 206,
        207, 209, 211. See also Eastern
        Church; Western Church
    conversion of Jews and, 226, 228
    corruption in, 211
Church Fathers, 92
Circumcision, 136–137, 208
Civilizations, ancient,
    of Assyrians, 14
    of Babylonia, 14
    of Egypt, 14
    of Hittites, 14
    of India, 14, 15
Clans
    of Hebrews, 114
Clement of Alexandria, 92
Codes of behavior. See Regulations,
        in Hinduism; in Judaism
Colonies
    of early Jews, 124

Conversion
    to Buddhism, 52, 102–103
        of Ashoka, 51
    to Christianity, 46, 195, 208, 214–
        216, 224–225
        of Constantine, 199–200, 202
        of Saxons, 196
    to Hinduism, 20
    to Islam, 45–46, 173, 183
        of Meccans, 163, 165
Communal worship, 36
Coomeraswamy, Ananda, 218
Companions
    of Muhammad, 166, 167, 177
Confession of Faith
    in Islam, 183
Congregation
    in Judaism, 131
Consciousness
    in Zen Buddhism, 95
Constantine
    conversion to Christianity of, 199–
        200, 209
Constantinople, 39
    emperor of, 209
Contemplative
    Muhammad as, 154
Corruption
    in Western Christianity, 198, 211
Cosmic Being
    in Hinduism, 30
Council of Nicea, 206
Covenant of God
    given to Abraham, 12, 106, 108, 109,
        122
    given to Moses, 122
    return to, 128
Cow
    as sacred symbol, 44–45
Cow Mother, 45
Creator. See also God; Prime Mover
    Hindu concept of, 17
    Jewish concept of, 110, 111
Creator of Happiness, 38
Creed
    of Islam, 183
Crucifixion, 133, 204, 219
    Buddhist reaction to, 219
Crusades, 133, 145
Cult
    of Krishna, 35
    of the river, 38

D

Damascus (Syria), 155, 163
Damma, See also Dharma
Dark Ages, 211
David, King, 119–121, 126, 170
    Ark of, 120–121

David, King (*continued*)
  death of, 120
  Jerusalem established as Israelite
    capital by, 120
Day of Atonement, 136
Dead Sea sects, 92
Decree of Toleration, 209
Delta
  of the Nile, 114
Dervishes, 182
Deuteronomy, 110, 122
  quotation from, 111
Devas, 62
Devi, 28
Dhamma, 85, 90
Dharma, 21
Dharma Bums, The, 93
Dhyana, 87, 96
Dialogue
  between Abraham and God, 106,
    108–109
  between Buddha and disciples, 75–
    77
  between Jews and God, 113
  between man and God, 2
  between Moses and God, 116
Diaspora, the, 124, 145, 199
Dietary laws
  in Hinduism, 15, 44–45
  in Judaism, 122, 136, 137–138
Dipankara, 55, 57
Disciples
  of Buddha, 71, 75–77, 77–78, 80, 90
Discourse on Fire, 76–77
Divine Ear, 87
Divine Essence, 112
Divine Eye, 87
Divine Ground of Being, 27
Divine origin
  of Hindus, 17
Divine Palace, 139
Divine Throne, 140
Doctrine. *See also* Islam, teachings
    of; Jesus, teachings of
  in Buddhism, 90–92. *See also*
    Buddha, Gautama, teachings of
Dreams
  of Buddha's mother, 57–58
  of Buddha's wife, 60
  of Constantine, 199, 200
  of Muhammad, 150
Du'a, 187
Durga, 28

E

Eastern Christianity, 196. *See also*
    Eastern Church; Eastern Or-
      thodox
  supernatural aspects of, 209

Eastern Church, 207, 209, 211. *See
    also* Eastern Christianity
Eastern Orthodox (Church), 207
Ecumenical Councils
  of Buddhists, 102
  of Christianity, 208, 209
Edict of Milan, 200
Egypt, 108
  flight of Jews from, 114
  migration of Jews to, 124
  sojourn of Jews in, 114
Eightfold Path, 71, 73, 75, 87
Elias, 170
Elijah, 170
Elijah of Vilna, 144
"Emancipation"
  of Western Jews, 147
Embodiment of the Supreme Spirit,
    38
Emirates, 169
Energizing Force, 84
Enlightened Being, 69, 85. *See also*
    "Buddha"; Buddha, Gautama;
    Enlightened One
Enlightened One, 69, 81, 96. *See also*
    "Buddha"; Buddha, Gautama;
    Enlightened Being
Enlightenment. *See also* Buddha-
    hood; Satori
  of Buddha's disciples, 76, 77, 78,
    82
  Fetters to, 89
Eno, 99
Enoch, 140
Epilepsy, 161, 162
Epistles, 204
Eucharist, the, 207, 219
Euphrates, 124
Exclusive religions, 214
Exile. *See* Babylonian Exile; Diaspora,
    the
Exodus, 124. *See also* Egypt, flight of
    Jews from
Extraordinary path
  of Hinduism, 22–23
Ezekiel, 121, 170
  Jewish mysticism, 139–140
Ezra, 170
  religious reforms and, 127–128

F

Faber, Felix, 116
Faith
  Christianity and, 220
Family life
  in India, 44
  Jews and, 137
Fasting
  by Buddha, 65, 66
  in Islam, 150, 183, 185

Father, the, 206, 207
Fatihah, 188
Fatima, 167
Feminine aspect
  of Hindu Cosmic Being, 30
Fetters
  to enlightenment in Buddhism, 89
Fifth caste, 17. *See also* Untouch-
    ables
Final Solution, 147
Fire
  Jewish mysticism and, 140
Fire Sermon, 76–77
First Ecumenical Council, 208
Five "Elements," 32
Five Pillars
  of Islam, 183
Five Supernatural Powers
  of Buddhism, 87, 89
Flower Generation, 93
Forbidden Zone
  of Mecca, 190
Force, Energizing, 84
Foucauld, Father Charles de, 224
Four Gospels, 204
Four Kings
  of the Four Quarters, 62
Four Signs
  of Buddhahood, 58–59
France
  spread of Islam to, 165

Hindu concept of, 24, 27–28, 30,
    33–34, 35–36, 112–113
Islamic concept of, 112, 154, 158,
    169–170
Jewish concept of, 110–113
  as supreme personal creator, 84
  of wrath and punishment, 1, 85
God Incarnate, 2
Goliath, 120
Good Friday
  liturgy of, 226
Gospels, 203, 204, 231
Govind (Hindu friend of author), 8,
    9, 11
Great Council
  of Buddha's disciples, 90
Great Enlightenment, 57
Greater Way, 91
Great Goddess, 30
Great Mother. *See* Kali
Great Raft, 91
Great Schism of 1054, 196
Great Wall of China, 165
Greeks
  Christianity and, 195
  in control of Judah, 129
  Islam and, 169
Green turban
  significance of, 191
Ground of All Being, 5
Guru, 22, 41, 144

G

Gabriel, 172. *See also* Angel Gabriel;
    Jibril
Gandhi, Mahatma, 17, 45, 46, 52, 118,
    223
  concept of Jesus and, 223–224
  quotation from, 233–234
Ganesh, 28
Ganges, 8, 38, 39, 40, 185
  mythical origin of, 38
  sacred names of, 38
Gaon, 144
Ganpatti, 28
Gas chambers
  of the Nazis, 110
Gaul, 199
"Gau Mata," 45
Gaza Strip, 149
Genesis, 106
  quotation from, 105
Ghat, 8, 39–40
Ghetto, 135, 136, 144
Gita, 34. *See also* Bhagavad Gita
God. *See also* Allah; Prime Mover
  Buddhist concept of, 84–85
  Christian concept of, 206–207

H

Hadath, 186
Hadith, 172
Hagar, 106, 156. *See also* Hajar
Hajar, 156. *See also* Hagar
  tomb of, 191
Hajj, 189–191. *See also* Pilgrimage
    to Mecca
Hajji, 191
Hanuman, 8, 9
Hanumanghat, 8
Hardwar, 38, 41
"Harijans", 17. *See also* Untouch-
    ables
Hasidic sects, 142
  in Brooklyn, N.Y., 143
  in conflict with established Juda-
    ism, 144
Hasidim, 142, 143–145
Heaven, 159. *See also* Paradise
Hebrew
  mysticism based on letters of, 142
Hebrews, 114. *See also* Israelites;
    Jews
Hejira, 163, 165
Hell, 159

Heretical sects
  of Christianity, 178, 200, 206, 209
  of Hinduism, 20
Hermit, 55. See also Recluse
  Buddha as, 64
  as sign of Buddhahood, 58
Herod, 203, 204
Herzl, Theodor, 145
Hidden Imam, 178
Himalayas, 38, 57
Hinayana (Buddhism), 91, 92
Hinduism, 1, 7–48, 225, 226
  concept of God in, 24, 27–28, 30,
    112–113
  concept of Jesus in, 221, 223
  conversion and, 19, 102
  Cosmic Being in, 30
  divine incarnations in, 221, 223
  influence on other religions of,
    15–16
  modern challenges to, 46–48
  pantheon of gods in, 9, 11, 24, 46
  relationship of caste system to, 16–
    17, 19
Hindu priests. See Brahmans
  divine origin of, 17
Hippie Generation, 93
His People, 109
Hittites, 14
Holy beggars, 65
Holy Days
  of Judaism, 136
Holy Ghost, the, 207. See also Holy
    Spirit
Holy Land, the, 118, 133, 145. See
    also Canaan; Israel; Palestine
Holy men
  in India, 67, 77. See also Bhikkhus;
    Holy beggars; Sadhus
Holy Spirit, the, 206
Horeb, Mount, 116
Household shrines
  in India, 36
House of Jacob, 114
Hud, 170
Hui-nēng, 99
Hui, Shen, 95
Hyksos
  dynasty of, 114

I

Ibn Saud, King, 190
Ibrahim, 156. See also Abraham
  sacrifice of Ismail by, 191
Iconography, 82
Idols
  in Islam, 156
Ignorance, 1, 84, 85
Imams, 178

Immigrants
  to Palestine, 145
Incarnations
  of Buddha, 57, 69
  in Christianity, 221, 223
  in Hinduism, 223
India
  Aryan Vedic period of, 30
  Christianity in, 215
  first Empire of, 51
  household shrines in, 36
  Islam in, 158, 215
  spread of Buddhism in, 91
Indonesia
  Christianity in, 215
Indulgences, 211
Inner Ruler, 24
Inquisition, the, 110
Intermarriage
  prohibition of, to Jews, 127–128
Iran, 175. See also Persia
Iraq, 167, 178
Isaac, 108, 109, 170
  sacrifice by Abraham of, 108–109,
    120
Isaiah, 126, 139
  book of, 113, 123
Isht Dev, 28
Ishwara Devi, 27–28
Islam
  abolition of caste and, 46
  almsgiving in, 183
  Buddhist influences on, 16
  concept of Christ in, 172
  concept of God in, 154–155, 158,
    169–170, 172
  conversion to, 45, 173
  creed of, 183
  after death of Muhammad, 166–169
  decline of Arab influence on, 169
  Five Pillars of, 183–191
  Hinduism and, 45–46
  pilgrimage to Mecca in, 183, 189–
    191
  prayer in, 185–189
  prophets in, 154, 170, 172
  ritual in, 183–191
  sacred literature of. See Qur'an
  secularization of, 167
  spread of, 158, 163, 165–166
  teachings of, 169–170, 172–173
Islamic world, 169
  position of women in, 174–177
Ismael, 106, 170. See also Ismail
  as founder of Arab peoples, 106,
    156
Ismail, 156. See also Ismael
  tomb of, 191
Israel, 110, 111, 113, 122, 123, 124,
    125. See also Canaan; Holy
    Land; Judah; Palestine; Zion

Israel (continued)
  fall of, 124
  people of, 124. See also Israelites; Jews
  present-day state of, 116, 131, 147
Israelites. See also Hebrews
  escape from Egypt by, 114
  pagan cults and, 119
  Torah given to, 116

J

Jacob, 109, 170
  House of, 114
Jains, 20
Japan
  Christianity in, 215
  spread of Buddhism in, 91
Jeddah, 189
Jeremiah, 139
Jerome, 92
Jerusalem, 39, 108, 132, 199
  capture of, 124
  destroyed by Romans, 129, 140, 199
  established as capital of Holy Land, 120
  Temple in, 120–121, 127
  walls rebuilt in, 127
Jesse, 126
Jesuits, 93
Jesus, 127, 195. See also Christ
  birth of, 204
  crucifixion of, 219
  death of, 204
  description of, 206
  Gandhi's ideas on, 223–224
  Hindu concept of, 221, 223
  as Islamic prophet, 172, 178, 230–231
  Jewish concept of, 226–231
  quoted in Qur'an, 172
  as Son of God, 206, 228, 229, 230
  teachings of, 233–234
  traditional view of, 206–207
Jews
  in America, 135–136
  as chosen People, 109–111
  concept of Trinity and, 207
  Christianity, and, 132–133, 135, 202–203, 208, 226, 228
  dispersal of, 124, 145, 199
  in Medina, 165
  as moneylenders, 133
  in Nazi Germany, 110, 147
  persecution of, 110–111, 132–133, 135, 142, 147
  in present-day Israel, 147
  Roman restrictions on, 132, 133
  sojourn in Egypt of, 113–114

Jhana, 87
Jibril, 150, 153, 154, 159, 162, 172
Jnana, 30
Job, 170
John the Baptist, 170
John of the Cross, St., 35
Joint family
  in India, 44
Jonah, 170
Jonathan, 119
Josaphat, Saint
  legend of, 92–93
Jordan, 150
Joseph, 114, 170
Judaeo-Christian tradition, 1
Judah, 124
  control by foreign powers of, 127–129, 131
  David as King of, 119–120
  fall of, 123
  reforms in, 127
Judah the Prince, 132
Judaism, 105–147
  in America, 135–136
  Buddhist influence on, 16
  concept of God in, 110–113
  dietary laws in, 122, 136, 137–138
  Hasidic movement in, 142–144
  importance of circumcision in, 136–137
  Judaeo-Christian sect within, 208
  modern challenge to, 147
  mysticism in, 139–140
  sacred literature of. See Talmud; Torah
  standardization of liturgy in, 131
  Zionism in, 145, 147

K

Ka'ba, 155–156, 189, 191
  idols of, 156, 190
Kali, 9, 28, 30, 32. See also Mahadevi
Kali Sutra, 32
Kaliyuga, 48
Kamala, Alara, 64
Kamma, 85–86. See also Karma
Kammic force, 86
Kapleau, Philip, 95
Karma, 20, 85. See also Kamma
Kartikeya, 30
Kasruth, 137–138
Kerouac, Jack, 93
Khadijah, 153, 159
Khalifates, 169
Khalifs, 166, 167
Khalifs, Righteous, 167, 177
Kings
  book of, 122

Knowledge of the Former States of Being
  perceived by Buddha, 69
Koran, 153, 225. *See also* Qur'an
Krishna, 24, 27, 30, 221
  cult of, 35
Kshatriyas, 17, 34, 59
Kufah, 163
Kundalini, 32

L

Lakshmi, 28
Lao-tzu, 90
Last Supper, the, 207
Latin, 90
Latin America
  Christianity in, 215, 225
Law, the, 116, 119. *See also* Torah
Laws. *See* Regulations
Legends. *See* Myths
Levites, 17
Leviticus
  book of, 122, 138
Lights, Blinding
  as Sufic images, 181
Lingam, 30
Literacy
  Judaism and, 128–129
Lithuania, 135
Little Raft, 91
Little Way, 91
Liturgy
  of Good Friday, 226
  of Judaism, 131
Lotuses, 57, 58
Lotus position, 9
Lubavitchers, 143–144
Luke, Saint, 204

M

Maccabean War, 203
Maccabees, 129
Ma Ganga, 38. *See also* Ganges
Magic
  in Hinduism, 33
  in Islam, 161–162, 169
  in Jewish mysticism, 140, 142
  in Tantric Buddhism, 91
Mahabharata, 34
Mahadevi, 30
Mahalasyapa, 96
Mahayana (Buddhism), 91
Mahdi, 178, 181
Mahendra, 52
Maimonides, Moses, 138
Manna, 116
Manu, 7

Mara the Fiend, 67. *See also* Mara
  the Temptress
Mara the Temptress, 62. *See also*
  Mara the Fiend
Marriage
  in Hinduism, 42, 44
  in Islam, 174–175
  in Judaism, 137
Masculine aspect
  of Hindu Cosmic Being, 30
Masutani, Fumio, 220
Master of the Good Name, 142
Maxentius, 199
Maya, Queen Maha, 57–58
Mecca, 39, 108, 149, 153, 156, 161, 167
  acceptance of Islam by, 165
  Forbidden Zone of, 190
  the Ka'ba in, 155, 189, 190, 191
  pilgrimage to, 183, 189–191
  return of Muhammad to, 163, 190,
    191
Medina, 161, 163, 165
  flight of Muhammad to, 161
  Jewish colony in, 163
  wars with Mecca and, 163
Meditation, 9, 41, 57
  in Buddhism, 87, 89
  by Gautama Buddha, 63–65
  by Muhammad, 154
  in Sufism, 181, 182
  in Zen Buddhism, 87, 89
Mediterranean Sea, 114, 124
Melkizadek, 120
Merkabah, 140, 142
Merton, Thomas, 95
Messenger of God, 173. *See also*
  Muhammad
Messiah, the, 124, 126–127
  Bar Kochba as, 209
  Christ as, 202–203, 209
  Islamic belief in, 178, 181
  Jewish belief in, 124, 126–127, 226,
    228
Methodists, 213
Micah, 122
  book of, 123
Michaux, Henri, 8–9
Middle Ages, 82
  Hasidic sects in, 142
Middle East
  Christianity in, 196
  Islam in, 158, 196
Middle Path. *See also* Middle Way
  of Buddhism, 73
Middle Way
  of Buddhism, 54, 84, 92
Migration
  of Aryans, 14–15, 19
Milan, Edict of, 200
Mina, 191
Minaret, 149

Miracles
  absence of, in Buddhism
  Baal Shem Tov and, 142–143
Mishnah, 132
Missionaries
  of Christianity, 93, 195, 208, 214,
    215, 216, 224–226
  of Hinduism, 46–47
Moghuls
  invasion of India by, 45–46
"Mohammedans," 225
Monasticism, 23, 92, 95
  in Buddhism, 100–102
  denial of, in Judaism, 137
Moneylenders, 133
Monotheism, 3, 27, 112, 154
Monsoons, 12
Mortification
  of the body, 64, 65–66, 73
Moscow, 39
Moses, 12, 114, 116, 170
Moslem. See Muslim
Mosque, 150, 187, 188
Mother Ganges, 38. See also Ganges
Mucalinda, 71
Muezzin, 149
Muhammad, 12, 153–155, 170, 172,
    173, 177
  birth of, 153
  Companions of, 166, 177
  death of, 165, 166
  early life of, 153
  Hejira of, 163
  Jibril and, 150, 153–154, 159, 162
  marriage of, 153–154
  Mecca and, 154, 156, 163
  Medina and, 161
  opposition to, 159, 161
  return to Mecca of, 163, 190, 191
  revelations of, 154, 161–163
  teachings of, 169–174
Murder
  of Jews by Crusaders, 133
  of Jews by Romans, 203
  of Jews by Nazis, 110
Muslims, 110, 149, 150, 153
  Christianity and, 230–231
  concept of the Trinity and, 207
  Holy Land and, 145
  Israel and, 147
  submission to Islam by, 150
Mysticism
  in Buddhism, 3, 4
  in Christianity, 3–4, 230
  in Hinduism, 3, 4
  in Islam, 3–4, 167, 181, 182
  in Judaism, 3–4, 12, 139–140
  Muhammad and, 161–162
Myths
  about Buddha, 81–82, 83
  about Christ, 82
  of Hinduism, 7, 38

N

Nabis, 170
Nahman of Bratslav, Rabbi, 137
Najasah, 186
Nazi Germany, 110
  Jewish refugees from, 147
Negev
  desert of, 108
Nehemiah
  as governor of Judah, 127–128
Nepal
  spread of Buddhism in, 91, 102
New Testament, 170, 195
Nibbana, 86. See also Nirvana
Nicea, Council of, 206
Nile
  delta of, 114
Niranja, 219
Nirvana, 54, 69, 71, 77, 78. See also
    Nibbana
Nivedita, Sister, 216, 218
Noah, 170
Noble Eightfold Path, 87. See also
    Eightfold Path
Nomads, 106, 109, 116
Nonviolence
  Gandhi and, 46
  Hinduism and, 20–21
North Africa
  Christianity in, 196, 215–216
  Islam in, 158, 196
Northern School
  of Buddhism, 91
North Star, the
  as symbol in Hindu marriage, 44
Numbers
  book of, 116

O

Occult
  in Tantric Buddhism, 91
Old Testament, 170
  Christ as theme of, 229
Omniscient Vision
  perceived by Buddha, 69
"On the Non-Existence of the Soul,"
    75
Oral tradition, 90. See also Myths
Origen, 92
Origin of Evil
  perceived by Buddha, 69
Orthodoxy
  in Christianity, 196–197, 207

Orthodoxy (*continued*)
in Hinduism, 82
in Islam, 177, 178, 179
in Judaism, 135–136, 145, 147

P

Paganism
Christianity and, 202, 208
Hinduism and, 4, 24. See also
Primordial religion, of India
Islam and, 156
Judaism and, 119
Pakistan
Islam in, 158, 215
Palestine, 145, 203
as British mandate, 131, 145
Palestinian Arabs, 147
Pali, 90, 93
Panchamas. See Untouchables
Pantheon
of Hindu gods, 9, 11, 24, 46
Papacy, 211, 213
Paradise, 155
Partisans, 178
Parvati, 28
Path
extraordinary, of Hinduism, 22–23
ordinary, of Hinduism, 21–22
Pauline mysticism, 230
Paul, Saint, 228, 229
Pentecost, 199
People of Determination, 170
People of Israel, 110. See also Chosen
People; Israelites; Jews
Perfect Enlightenment, 69. See also
Buddhahood; Enlightenment
Persecution
of Christians, 209
of Jews, 110–111, 132–133, 135, 142,
147
Persia, 158, 195. See also Iran
Shi'a as official version of Islam
in, 178
Persians, 129, 169
"Personal" gods
of Hinduism, 27–28
Peter, 198–199, 211
Pilgrimage, 64
to Benares, 39–41
to Mecca, 183, 189–191
rite of 'umra as, 163
to sacred rivers, 36, 38
Plural marriage
in Islam, 175
Pogroms, 110
Poland, 135
"Polished Mirror," 89
Pollution
by Untouchables, 17, 47

Polytheism
in Hinduism, 9, 24, 46
Pope, the, 209
Pope John XXIII, 226
Position of women
in Hindu society, 20
in Islamic society, 174–175, 177
Prajna, 99
Prayer
in Hinduism, 36, 38, 40–41
in Islam, 149–150, 161, 183, 185–189
in Judaism, 135, 140, 143
Prayer rug, 149
Predestination, 86
Presbyterians, 213
Priestly caste. See Brahmans
Priests
role in Judaism of, 128, 135
in Hinduism. See Brahmans
Prime Mover, 4
Primordial religion
of India, 15, 48
Prince of Peace, 126
Promised Land, 114, 118. See also
Canaan; Israel; Zion
Propagation. See also Missionaries;
Proselytizing
of Buddhism, 90–91
by Jewish prophets, 121–122
Prophet, the, 149, 153, 191. See also
Muhammad
successors of, 166–167
Prophets
of Islam, 154, 170
of Israel, 121–123, 124, 126, 139–140,
228
Proselytizing. See also Missionaries;
Propagation
by Christians, 154
by Jews, 154
Protestantism, 46, 207, 213–214
Psalms, 120, 123
Psychic Powers, 87, 89
Pure Abodes, 89
Purgatory, 211
Purification
in Islam, 186–187

Q

Qiblah, 187
Qur'an, 153, 162, 165, 166, 170, 172,
173, 174, 187, 188, 190. See also
Koran
quotations from, 162, 163, 165, 166,
173, 174

R

Rabbis, 132
entrance to heaven of, 140
in Hasidic sect, 144–145

Radhakrishnan, Sarvepalli, 218, 220–221

Raka'h, 188

Ramadan, 150, 183, 185

Ramakrishna, 22
  Order of, 221

Rama, Lord, 8

Rashi of Troyes, 118

Rebbes (leaders), 143

Rebirth. *See also* Reincarnation
  Buddhist concept of, 64, 65, 76, 77, 85–87, 89
  Hindu concept of, 15, 19, 41

"Recital, The," 150, 153

Recluses, 41. *See also* Hermit

Red Sea, the, 114, 155

Reform movements
  in Christianity, 211
  in Hinduism, 46
  in Judaism, 145

Regulations
  in Hinduism, 15, 44–45. *See also* Caste system; Ritual, in Hinduism
  in Islam, 183–191
  in Judaism, 122, 131–132, 143. *See also* Kasruth; Torah

Reincarnations, 15, 19, 21. *See also* Rebirth
  of Buddha, 57

Religious freedom
  of Jews in Medina, 163

Reminiscence of Past Births, 87

Resort of the Eminent, 38

Resurrection of Christ, 208

Revelations
  experienced by Muhammad, 154, 159–163
  of Islamic prophets, 170–173

Revolt
  by Jews against Romans, 129

Right Concentration, 87

Righteous Imam, 178

Righteous Khalifs, 167, 177

"The Righteous one of God," 178

Riots
  against Jews, 133. *See also* Pogroms

Ritual
  in Buddhism, 101–102
  in Christianity, 207–208, 219
  in Hinduism, 21–22, 28, 33, 36, 42, 44, 85
  in Islam, 149, 183, 186–188, 191
  in Judaism, 136, 137–138, 208

Rivers
  as centers of worship, 36, 38, 39–41

"The Rock upon which I found my Church," 211

Roman Catholicism, 207, 211, 212, 214
  in Latin America, 216

Roman Empire
  Christianity in, 132, 133, 135, 195, 199–200
  division of, 132, 209
  restrictions on Jews in, 132–133

Romans, 39, 110, 145, 199
  control of Judah by, 129, 203
  Jewish revolts against, 209
  occupation of Palestine by, 203

Rosenzweig, Franz, 113

Russia
  Christianity in, 196
  pogroms in, 110

S

Sacraments. *See also* Ritual
  absence in Buddhism of, 84
  in Christianity, 207–208
  in Hinduism, 42, 44

Sacred cow, 44–45

Sacred Literature
  of Christianity. *See* Bible
  of Hinduism, 32–33. *See also* Bhagavad Gita; Upanishads; Vedas
  of Islam. *See* Qur'an
  of Judaism. *See* Talmud; Torah

Sadhus, 19, 22. *See also* Bhikkus; Holy men, of India

St. John of the Cross, 35

Sakti, 28

Sakyamuni, 54

Sakyas, 54, 57

Salah, 186

Sala trees, 219

Salih, 170

Samadhi, 87

Samskaras, 42

Sanctity of life
  to Hindus, 44–45. *See also* Nonviolence

Sangha, 102

Sannyasin, 23

Sanskrit, 90, 93

Sarah, 106, 108

Sarai, 106

Samath, 8
  Deer Park at, 71

Satori, 98, 100

Saxons
  conversion of, 196

Saul, King, 119

Saviour, 203. *See also* Messiah
  Buddhist concept of, 83, 221

Scandinavia
  Christianity in, 196

Scriptures. *See also* Sacred Literature
  in Buddhism, 100

Scriptures (*continued*)
  in Hinduism, 11, 19
  in Judaism, 131, 132
Search for God, 2, 24, 27
Sechem, 106
Second Coming of Christ, 172, 226
  Islamic belief in, 181
Secularism
  in Islam, 167
  in Judaism, 110–111, 136, 147
"Seed"
  of Abraham, 105, 106
Sermon on the Mount
  influence of, on Gandhi, 46
"Setting in Motion the Wheel of the
  Law, etc.,'' 71
Seven sacred cities
  of India, 38, 71
Sexual cults, 28
Shahs, 178
Shahadah, 183
Sha, Hüen, 100
Shakti, 30, 32
Shalom, 120
Shekkinah, 111
Shi'a, 178, 179
Shibayama, Zenkei, 95
Shi'ites, 178
Shiva, 9, 11, 28, 30, 38, 39
  cults of, 30
Shivaites, 30
Shruti, 32
Shu'ayb, 170
Siddartha, Gautama, 54, 58–60, 62.
  See also Buddha, Gautama
Sikkim, 102
Sin
  in Hinduism, 19–20
  in Judaism, 113
Sinai
  peninsula of, 114, 116, 118
Sin-destroying, 38
Slaughter
  of animals, 138–139
Slavery, 14, 51
  of Jews in Egypt, 114, 137
Smirti, 32, 34
Snake King, 71
Solomon, 120, 121, 170
  Temple of, 121
Somalia, 177
Song of God, the, 34. *See also*
  Bhagavad Gita
Son of God. *See also* Christ
  Jesus as, 206, 228, 229, 230
Soul
  and rebirth, 41, 65
Southeast Asia
  spread of Buddhism in, 91

Southern School
  of Buddhism, 91
Spanish Inquisition, 110
Staircase to Heaven, 38
Standing, the, 188
Submission
  to Islam, 150
  of Meccans, 163
Successor
  of the Messenger of God, 166
Suddhodana, King, 57, 60, 62–63, 66
Sudras, 17
Suffering
  Buddhist attitudes toward, 54, 73,
    75, 219
  Christian attitudes toward, 219
Sufis, 172, 181–182
  quotation from poetry of, 182–183
Sultanates, 169
Sumedha, 55, 57
Sun
  as sacred symbol of Hinduism, 39,
    40, 113
Sunnah, 177
Sunnis, 177
Superstition. *See also* Magic
  in Buddhism, 84, 102
  in Islam, 169
Supreme Brahman, 64
Supreme Power
  absence in Buddhism of concept of,
    85
Supreme Wisdom
  in Zen Buddhism, 99
Surahs, 162, 188
Suzuki, D. T., 219–220
Symbolism
  in Christianity, 200, 219
  in Hinduism, 38–40, 44–45, 113
Syria, 153, 155
  control of Judah by, 129

T

Talmud, the, 123, 132
  study of, 135, 144
Tantric Buddhism, 91
Taureg, 224
Tehran (Iran), 149
Tel Aviv (Israel), 131
Temple, the, 120–121, 128
  mystical concept of, 131–132
Temptation
  of Buddha, 67
Ten Commandments, 109, 122
Ten Perfections
  of Buddhahood, 57
Thathagata, 84–85
Theosophists, 3
Thien, 96

Thomas, 208
Thought Reading, 87, 89
Three Baskets
  of Buddhist doctrine, 90
"Those who submit," 150
Three Characteristics
  of Buddhist life, 89
Three Pillars of Zen, 95
Throne of God, 139
Tiberius Caesar, 204
Tibetan, 93
Tibet
  spread of Buddhism in, 91
Tigris, 124
Tirtha, 38
Tithes, 139
Tolerance, 4
Tong, Tran Thia, 100–101
Torah, the, 116, 123, 131, 132, 136,
  140
  commentary on. *See* Talmud
  mystic concept of, 128
  return to, 128
  revised code of, 128
  study of, 135, 144
Tosu, 96, 98
Tradition
  in Hinduism, 36
Traditions
  in Islam, 172–173
  in Judaism, 131. *See also* Talmud
Transjordan, 165
Tribal gods
  in Islam, 154
Trinity, the, 207
  reaction of Jews and Muslims to,
  207
Tripitaka, 90
Truc Lam, the Venerable, 101
Truth
  received by Buddha, 71, 78
Tse, Teu, 100
Turkey, 190
Turks, 169
Twelvers, the, 178

U

Uma, 28
Umayyads, 167
'Umra
  rite of, 163
Untouchables
  conversion to Buddhism by, 17, 47
  pollution of caste Hindus by, 17
Upanishads, 34
Uruvela, 66, 71
Usury, 159. *See also* Moneylenders

V

Vaisayas, 17
"Vassa," 77
Vedas, 32, 33, 46, 47
Vedic Aryans, 14, 30
Vedic period
  in India, 34
Vietnam, 100
Vishnu, 14, 30, 35, 48

W

Warfare
  Buddhism and, 52
  Christianity and, 200, 202, 207
  Hinduism and, 44. *See* Nonviolence
  Islam and, 163, 165
Warrior caste. *See* Kshatriyas
Way, the (to Buddhahood), 101. *See
    also* Eightfold Path; Greater
    Way; Little Way; Middle Way
Wazirs, 167
Western Christianity, 209, 211. *See
    also* Protestantism; Roman Ca-
    tholicism; Western Church
  reform movement in, 211
Western Church, 209. *See also* Protes-
    tantism; Roman Catholicism;
    Western Christianity
Western religion
  Christianity as, 215–216
Wilderness
  Baal Shem Tov in, 142–143
  Jews' forty years in, 114, 116
Women
  position in Hindu society of, 20
  position in Islamic society of, 174–
  177
Wonderful Counselor, 126
World view
  of Buddhism, 1
  of Christianity, 2
  of Hinduism, 1
  of Islam, 2
Wudu, 187

Y

Yasodhara, 59, 60, 62
Yemen, 155
Yen Tu, Mount, 101
Yireh, 120
Yogananda, Paramahansa, 22
Yogi, 41
Yom Kippur, 136

Z

Zakat, 183
Zachariah, 126, 170
Zeddiks, 144
Zen Buddhism, 87, 91, 92–103
 influence on West of, 93, 103

masters of, 95, 98, 100
nonverbal quality of, 96
spread of, 98
Zion, 118, 126, 145. *See also* Israel
Zionist Congress, 145
Zoroastrians, 165 •
 influence on Islam of, 178

ABOUT THE AUTHOR

EDWARD RICE is a writer, artist and photographer who has traveled extensively throughout the Middle East, Southern Asia, East Africa, Latin America and the South Pacific. Mr. Rice is the author of *The Man in the Sycamore Tree: The Good Times and Hard Life of Thomas Merton, Mother India's Children* and *The Church: A Pictorial History*.